The Traveling Photographer

ANN AND CARL PURCELL

AMPHOTO
An Imprint of Watson-Guptill Publications/New York

To each other
and
Kurt and Gladys Frederick

Edited by Robin Simmen
Designed by Bob Fillie
Graphic production by Stanley Redfern

First published 1988 in New York by AMPHOTO,
an imprint of Watson-Guptill Publications,
a division of Billboard Publications, Inc.,
1515 Broadway, New York, NY 10036

Library of Congress Cataloging-in-Publication Data
Purcell, Ann.
   The traveling photographer.
   Includes index.
   1. Travel photography.   I. Purcell, Carl.   II. Title.
TR790.P87   1988   778.9′991   88-10541
ISBN 0-8174-6200-7
ISBN 0-8174-6201-5 (pbk.)

Manufactured in Japan

1 2 3 4 5 6 7 8 9 / 96 95 94 93 92 91 90 89 88

Contents

Introduction

This portrait of an elderly tribal woman in southern China is accented nicely by the sunlight on her face. The right side of the picture is dark, providing a simple, uncluttered background for the woman's profile.

Travel has stimulated the intellectual curiosity of creative people for centuries. Writers and painters have always recorded and documented their adventures in words and pictures, but it was the advent of the camera that allowed travelers to accurately and literally share their experiences with others. Photography offered travelers a way to conveniently preserve and catalog their visual memories. In the early days the awkward task of working with a view camera on a tripod was the only option for a traveler on the move. Today's 35mm single-lens-reflex (SLR) camera allows the travel photographer to carry a whole camera system in one shoulder bag, and makes it possible to transport picture viewers to the far corners of the world.

Any picture that captures and interprets the unique qualities of a location can be called a travel photograph. In fact, most photographs naturally fall into this category. Even your own hometown is someplace new to an outsider. People usually think of travel photography in terms of calendar scenics, but actually, that is a very narrow definition. Travel photography can and should include many subjects such as people, art, food, recreation, and architecture. These are the details that reflect the essence and culture of a region so they are all elements needed for a comprehensive coverage of a destination. The photographer must utilize color and light. He or she needs to be aware of graphic design in creating compositions on the canvas of imagination.

A romantic mystique swirls around professional travel photographers, but we are in fact, just like all photographers who pursue the common goal of outstanding pictures. Amateurs and pros use the same type of photographic equipment. The major difference between them is that professionals pursue their art for profit, while amateurs shoot strictly for pleasure. We chose to become professional travel photographers and work as a team because, as husband and wife, we wanted to be together. In addition, we felt we could complement each other's talents and energies in a highly competitive field.

The lives we lead are enviable. Photography has taken us to exotic locations around the world, to isolated and adventurous places as well as to the playgrounds of the rich and famous. We've been hang gliding over Rio, scuba diving on Australia's Great Barrier Reef, swimming with dolphins in the Florida Keys, and chasing elephants on the plains of East Africa. Our assignments have included recording rainbows in Ireland, riding the Glacier Express from St. Moritz to Zermatt, exploring the burning sands of the Gobi desert, and spending the night in an underwater hotel.

Many capable and creative photographers wistfully dream about an assignment from a top travel magazine to go to the South Pacific and shoot the ultimate picture layout. Ideally, they hope to be sent first class with an assistant and be paid $1,500 a day to spend twenty-two days in paradise. We hate to dampen anyone's enthusiasm, but such editorial assignments just don't exist. Day rates for a leading travel magazine such as *National Geographic* or *Travel & Leisure* vary, but an average rate might be four-hundred dollars per day for a top photographer. Only a handful of elite professionals receive such assignments. High-pay advertising assignments are even tougher to get. Then, where do the assignments for travel photographers originate?

Magazines, advertising agencies, public-relations firms, corporations, airlines, hotel chains, and international banks hand out well-paid photography assignments every day. The results, often impressive, glossy, and sophisticated, appear in ads, newspapers, magazines, books, and even on television. The results are often impressive and visually sophisticated. Today's audience lives in a visually oriented culture and expects to see everything illustrated by outstanding pictures in full color. Clearly, a world of commercial opportunities awaits the ambitious travel photographer.

Relatively few photographers concentrate on coming up with good ideas. Editors and art directors are always on the lookout for creative suggestions, and if you can come up with one that appeals to the right person, you may find yourself with an assignment. Suppose you're going to Bangkok, Thailand, on a business trip or vacation. You read through the guidebooks and come across a mention of the floating markets on the "klongs," or canals. At first glance this appears to be a good subject, but on further research you discover it has been photographed and published many times before. The idea isn't so good!

On the other hand you may find an obscure reference to the giant, hand-painted movie billboards in Bangkok. These enormous bill-

We researched and photographed the subject of hand-painted movie billboards in Bangkok, Thailand as a self-assigned project and later sold it as a magazine feature. This picture is now part of the permanent American Society of Magazine Photographers collection at the George Eastman House in Rochester.

During an assignment in Rio de Janeiro, we went hang gliding over the city. The flight over Rio (top left) was breathtaking and provided us with excellent aerial views. For shots from the hang glider, we used a full-frame fisheye lens set at infinity.

We have often explored the underwater world with our cameras. While we were being certified as divers, we wrote and provided pictures about diver certification for Diversion *magazine. This shot (bottom left) was made near St. Thomas in the U.S. Virgin Islands.*

boards, often towering three stories high, are a unique art form depicting humor, passion, and pathos, and are painted in giant sections in studio lofts. Now this is an unusual idea for travel pictures, but before you rush off to buy a ticket to Bangkok, we should mention that we sold this picture feature a number of years ago to *TWA Ambassador* magazine.

Scanning newspapers and magazines is an excellent way to come up with good picture ideas. You may see a short news item or a brief feature—one without pictures—that will give you a terrific idea. Put together a clip file of such ideas and use them to query editors or shoot the story on your own.

It is also important to direct your photographic efforts toward a specific goal. Most travelers with a camera simply shoot as they go

along, which leads to slipshod coverage. The successful travel photographer decides ahead of time what statement the pictures should make and whether they will present a theme or a subject. After the goal is determined, the photographer must impose the necessary discipline to achieve it. For example, in the case of the movie billboards in Bangkok we had to set aside enough time to do the shooting during our visit there. We made inquiries to locate the various art studios where these billboards were produced, and we set up appointments at these locations. Fortunately, we did not need to bring elaborate lighting since most of the studios had skylights or big windows. In addition, we traveled to major movie theaters throughout Bangkok to photograph the billboards on display and documented the interesting juxtaposition

You might assign yourself to do a series of pictures of Paris at night. This picture of the Arc de Triomphe on the Champs-Elysée could be included in such a series. The time exposure was made using a cable release and tripod with daylight color film. Notice that the headlights and taillights of moving cars were recorded as red-and-white streaks.

of diminutive Thai people walking beneath gargantuan illustrations of oriental movie stars. The point is that it takes planning and effort to execute a photographic project, even when it is self-assigned.

When you select a photographic goal or give yourself an assignment, your objective can be broad or narrow, as ours was in Bangkok. On a trip to Paris you might be motivated to shoot the illuminated monuments and buildings of "the city of light" after dark. With a tripod you can make short time exposures of the Arc de Triomphe with the swirling traffic on the Champs-Elysées, the flood-lit Eiffel Tower, and the illuminated cathedral of Notre Dame. The theme of "Paris Monuments at Night" ties these images together, and if you add historical facts and figures about each structure and obtain further information about the cost of the electricity that illuminates the monuments and buildings, you've then created a first-class feature package ready to be published.

In very practical terms beginning photographers must make their own assignments and cover their own expenses. These constraints occasionally apply to photographers who have established reputations and reflect the reality of a highly competitive field of work. However, this also keeps the door open for talented beginners who are willing to invest their own money and time in projects they want to pursue.

Travel photography is not a closed shop. If you have a good idea for doing picture coverage of a nearby town, the next state, or anywhere in the world, try for an assignment. If you can't get one, go ahead and do it anyway. If your idea and pictures are good enough and if you follow the marketing guidelines provided in this book, your package should eventually sell.

Many amateur photographers are interested in knowing how they can create some additional income from their relatively expensive hobby. Traveling photographers should always be aware of the potential pictures have for stock sales, both directly and through picture agencies. Over the years we have built a stock file of approximately 350,000 color slides shot in ninety-one countries. These pictures produce a substantial income for us. In the last chapter of this book we describe how the amateur as well as the aspiring professional can increase his or her income through stock sales.

Not all our readers are interested in selling their pictures and making a profit. Many photographers shoot only for their own pleasure or to share their pictures with their friends. If this is your intent, you still need to define your photographic goals: try to establish a mood or feeling and convey as well the necessary visual information about your theme or subject.

Travel photographers don't measure success in terms of money because very few photographers become wealthy in this field. Most of our satisfaction comes from creating exciting images of interesting places, but part of our motivation is just to see new places and exchange ideas with people from other cultures. If we didn't travel to take pictures, we would travel for some other reason. Creating a successful reputation in travel photography depends on sweat and talent, but we've been willing to work from sunrise to sunset and often spend just as much time captioning and marketing our pictures. As practical professional photographers, we are pleased that our travel pictures are widely published in major magazines, calendars, posters, and coffee-table books, but we also have to satisfy ourselves. Many of our favorite pictures have never sold and may never be published, but taking them has given us great pleasure and we've enjoyed ourselves along the way.

Travel is the fulfillment of many people's dreams, and our work illustrates the fairy tales of life. Ideally, the world is a beautiful place, so, like Don Quixote, we have chosen to search for the quintessence of the impossible dream in our approach to travel photography. This dream of beauty is elusive and fleeting. Capturing it on film requires long hours working behind the viewfinder. Not

We shot this picture of a brass-helmeted, horse-mounted guard in London on an overcast day. Koda-chrome 64 provided a nice rendition of the skin tone and accurately re-corded the crimson of the guard's coat. The picture's dark background concentrates attention on the figure and accents the balanced composition.

Outstanding pictures often happen in a fleeting moment. We stepped into the mouth of this colorful hot-air balloon (top left) as it was being deflated in Albuquerque, New Mexico. The tiny figures of the ground crew were unexpectedly silhouetted against the billowing nylon envelope. We had only enough time for three quick shots using a motor drive with the camera set in the program-exposure mode.

Graphic designs can often be found in nature. The stripes on these zebras (bottom left) resemble lines drawn with india ink. The configuration of three bodies and a single head is an interesting mixture of realism and abstract design.

all travel photographers focus on the positive, upbeat aspects of the world they discover away from home, but we delight in seeing the positive side of life. We are selective about what we photograph and usually try to show the most attractive aspects of a country or city. The pure photojournalist or documentary photographer often has a different and more complex purpose.

We strive to give the people who see our pictures a vicarious sense of being where we were. This lets viewers share the beauty and charm of a place even if they can never go there. At the same time, we consciously try to preserve the realism inherent in an image. We prefer to photograph the world as we find it, giving our particular interpretation of the subject through its relation to light and various angles.

Most good photographs are very simple and straight forward. Manipulating the subject is a perfectly valid part of photography, but our primary love is for the natural, unaltered image. So much can be expressed simply by choosing one lens over another or waiting for the decisive moment to take the picture.

The manipulation of photography can be done through trick filters, multiple exposures, sandwiched transparencies, and solarizations. We are cautious about overusing these techniques and try not to destroy the basic integrity of a photographic image. Fortunately, the camera isn't a tool flexible enough to allow extensive alteration of the basic image, but all photographers should also be concerned with what happens after a picture has been exposed and sent elsewhere for publication. Although computerized digital imagery can be used for creative purposes, it is now possible in post-production to create what was not actually there. Seeing an incorrect caption with your work can be upsetting, but it would be even worse if a technician at a computer alters your picture's visual reality. While enhancing photographs may be valid, changing information and content is not.

In the end, cameras don't take pictures; people do. Cameras are just inert blocks of metal and optical glass interlaced with complex electronic circuits. Great photographs are created in the mind of the photographer whose eye recognizes the beauty of a fleeting moment, the graceful curve of a sun-washed beach, or the morning mist rising from a forest glen. Creative photographers utilize skill, color, and light to translate what the eye sees through the lens of a camera onto the film's emulsion. This obviously requires a mastery of equipment and a certain level of technical skill. However, automatic and autofocus camera systems have put photography within the reach of nontechnical people who have the talent to recognize a good picture. Fortunately, most SLR cameras, including those with autofocus lenses, also permit the option for manual operation.

Some photographers are understandably reluctant to share their professional secrets or freely offer their formulas for success. Aspiring travel photographers need this information, however, and that is why we decided to write this book. Many aspects of travel photography are covered here, including life on the road, creative and technical problems, how to market stock images and deal with editors and agencies, bookkeeping, and filing. The following photo essays about shooting on location in Paris, London, Bali, Prince Edward Island, China, and East Africa demonstrate the importance of being aware of all these aspects before you leave home.

Essentially, this book is a blueprint for how to succeed in travel photography as an art and as a business. If you are serious about doing travel photography as an amateur or hope to turn this hobby into a profitable enterprise as a part-time or full-time professional, this book will show you how to do it. The first requirement is to find the motivation and the drive. If you love travel and love photography, you're well on the road to using your camera as a passport to adventure.

OF all the places in the world, our favorite spring-time destination is Paris. It is a city filled with light, art, and food, a visual feast for photographers. Its vast green parks, broad boule-vards, elegant women promenading along the Champs-Elysées, and chil-dren playing in the shadow of Notre Dame all create an inspiring parade of images. As you stroll through Paris, it is easy to understand how this bright, sparkling city inspired the Impres-sionist painters. Sunshine filters through new leaves and old trees, spilling patches of gold and green across the soft surface of park lawns. Paris is appro-priately named "The City of Light."

The Arc de Triomphe is a fine place to start on a photographic walk through this exciting city in the spring. Victorious armies have marched through this mighty archway, but today it is often a gateway for flocks of pigeons on their way home to roost. On a warm spring night you can

set up your tripod on one of the traffic islands in the Champs-Elysées. We advise shooting with a slow slide film, such as daylight Koda-chrome 64, at an opening of about f/8 with a cable release to avoid any camera movement. During the day you can take an elevator to the top of this monument for an impressive view of Paris from above.

From this massive arch-way, you can take a lei-surely walk down the Champs-Elysées to observe and photograph the French at their leisure as they walk their poodles or sip Pernod and water at a sidewalk cafe. The walk to the Place de la Concorde (top right) and the Tuileries is a long one, but quite pleasant in the spring. The latter royal park is a haven of green glass and trees, a place where children sail colorful toy sailboats in large ponds and families picnic on the cool expanses of lawn.

The Louvre, an en-lightened art museum (bot-tom right) that allows handheld photography

without electronic flash, is located at the far end of Tuileries. On a sunny day the Louvre has sufficient light from windows and skylights for you to use Kodachrome 200 to take indoor pictures of paintings, sculpture, and other art lovers. Recording great masterpieces in a fraction of a second is literally a snap. It is even more fascinating to use your camera to catch people reacting to the art.

There are a few vantage points for photographing Paris. You might ride to the top of Monsieur Eiffel's folly or climb Notre Dame's tortuous, winding staircase to stroll among the demonic gargoyles. Such activities are not recommended for photographers suffering from acrophobia but can be exhilarating on a beautiful spring weekend. Looking down from the ramparts of Notre Dame (shown here at night), you'll have a fabulous view of the Seine River. Divided by the flying buttresses of Notre Dame, the Seine forms a cradle of history. Barges and sightseeing boats trace patterns on its grey-green water while vendors sell books, prints, and colorful balloons at riverside stalls in the Bohemian atmosphere of the Left Bank.

We think you'll agree that Paris is the most romantic city in the world. Go there in the spring with your cameras and you'll bring back images that will warm your heart on a winter night.

LONDON

LONDON is a friendly, civilized city and a great place to take pictures. Samuel Johnson said, "When a man is tired of London, he is tired of life". For a photographer, this stimulating city is never boring and is filled with visual variety and interest at every turn.

Where you stay in London often dictates where you take pictures. In the West End theater district we like the Marlborough Crest, but around Harrod's the old and luxurious Hyde Park Hotel is pleasantly reminiscent of the reign of Queen Victoria. There are also a wide variety of budget-priced bed-and-breakfast rooms near Victoria Station. If you like the idea of dining with the photojournalists, writers, and lawyers of Fleet Street, we highly recommend The Wig and Pen, a private club open to foreign travelers. Make reservations through your hotel concierge.

London has established certain traditions. Having tea in the Palm Court at the Ritz Hotel on the edge of Green Park is a delightful way to end a busy after-noon of shopping. One day, after leaving a trail of credit-card slips through the Burlington Arcade, we arrived at the Ritz around four o'clock, having worked up our thirst for steaming cups of Earl Grey and buttered crumpets. Imagine our disappointment at being politely, but firmly, turned away. Gentlemen are required to wear jackets and ties, and women should be quietly elegant. We made reservations to come back two days later.

Head waiter Michael Twomey explained the reasons for the dress code. "The Ritz Palm Court is a stage, and we do insist on certain dress rules: jacket and ties for gentlemen and no jeans or sneakers. I would like it very much if ladies still wore hats for tea." The British cling to tradition, and tea at the Ritz is one of those traditions.

Photographing London calls for a combination of walking and public transportation. Piccadilly Circus (top left) and the West End is considered the center with easy walks to Buckingham Palace, Trafalgar

Square, the Strand, and Green Park. You may want to use a taxi or the tube to go to Fleet Street, Harrod's, and Hyde Park. Try taking pictures of people feeding the pigeons in Trafalgar Square under the stern scrutiny of Lord Nelson standing atop his lofty column. This is also a good site for night pictures with a tripod since the fountains in the square and the National Portrait Gallery are illuminated at night (shown left). Another popular location for pictures is Westminster Bridge with its excellent view of the clock tower housing Big Ben. Of course, no one wants to miss the changing of the guard at Buckingham Palace (below), but with today's crowds, this is becoming an increasingly difficult subject for good pictures. Instead, we suggest you photograph the changing of the horse guard at the Admiralty Building, where you can still get excellent closeups of the proper young guards wearing black bearskin hats.

Part of London's visual interest lies in its architec-ture. The city's ancient buildings are steeped in history. Traveling photographers are usually awed by such impressive structures as Westminster Abbey, Parliament, St. Paul's Cathedral, and the Tower of London but may be uncertain about the best way to record them photographically. Although every building presents different photographic problems, a common problem with buildings in London is linear distortion (see "Architecture" in chapter 3). London's narrow streets make using a perspective-control (PC) lens the best way to correct this distortion.

The 70-210mm zoom lens is a good tool for picking out architectural details such as gargoyles, turrets, door knockers, and leaded-glass windows. London is filled with such examples of architectural whimsy, and a walk through the quiet side streets of Mayfair is a journey of discovery. The spotmeter available on Minolta and Olympus cameras comes in handy here, allowing you to take ex-posure readings of very small areas in the frame for pinpoint exposures. (A handheld spotmeter can be used if you don't have these particular cameras.) Remember, however, that using the exposure setting recommended by a spot reading of a shadow area often washes out the highlighted areas in the picture.

Aside from old buildings, London is filled with friendly people who combine tradition and individualism and whose personalities sometimes border on the eccentric. Although George Bernard Shaw observed that Americans and the English are a people divided by a common language, speaking a common language is an advantage for a photographer when asking a stranger to pose for a picture. From retired army officers to punk rockers, the English are surprisingly cooperative when it comes to pictures. Prime places for people pictures are Piccadilly Circus, Covent Gardens, Speaker's Corner at Hyde Park, and the Portobello Road Flea Market on Sundays.

BALI is the definitive island of the South Pacific. Like the early Dutch explorers, we fell in love with this lush tropical island, washed clean by the monsoon rains and cooled by the persistent ocean breeze. Broad beaches and volcanic mountains make Bali an idyllic physical environment, the perfect paradise we all dream about. This lovely setting provides a spectacular backdrop for pictures, but it is the people of Bali who offer the best subjects for photography. They are gentle and sweet, open to personal contact, and usually delighted to pose for pictures.

We stopped our car on an isolated mountain road near the center of the island. A village woman with three children was walking along the road, a basket of goods balanced gracefully on her head and an infant son cradled in her arms. Her two daughters walked beside her, each carrying a

bundle of wood in the traditional manner. With a 200mm lens we recorded this scene from another century. The grace, poise, and dignity of the woman made an unforgettable image, frozen in time and preserved in our cameras. Our guide asked the woman to pose for us, and she shyly agreed, allowing us to get intimate closeups with a shorter zoom lens.

The Bali Sol Hotel where we stayed was part of an elaborate resort complex. The hotel and surrounding gardens reflected the island culture and architecture with considerable taste. The gardens, filled with high stands of bamboo and elaborate reflecting ponds with delicate lotus blossoms, offered some fine picture possibilities. A wide-angle lens provided a sweeping sense of the tropical gardens while our macro lenses let us get within inches of vivid hibiscus blossoms. You could almost be seduced by the comfort and beauty of such a hotel, but remember that this is an artificial environment. The most valid photographic potential of Bali exists in the villages and the lush countryside. You should make the effort to get off the hotel grounds and find these images.

Rental cars are available, but we recommend a car with a driver/guide who can speak English. To reach the countryside you'll probably have to drive through the crowded resort areas and even the capital city of Denpasar. These areas are difficult to negotiate under the best conditions with pedicabs, motor scooters, and children darting into the crowded streets. The uninitiated driver, forced to adhere to the left side of the narrow road, will find driving difficult. Most hotels have a Bali Tours and Travel desk and the daily rates are quite reasonable.

We would also urge the visiting photographer to get out of the car to explore the villages and jungles of Bali. We walked along a jungle path and it was like walking into the canvas of a Rousseau painting. The vines and trees seemed more like products of imagination than nature. The path led to the ruins of a Hindu temple, overgrown with vines and covered with green moss. It was a sacred place haunted by the presence of ancient gods; flower petals and charred incense were still on the altar. Nearby, a giant banyan tree stretched its aerial roots downward, seeking the sustenance of the moist earth. A spirit house had been constructed in the upper branches to harbor the wandering souls of revered ancestors.

The people of Bali celebrate death as enthusi-

astically as they celebrate life. We were invited to a traditional cremation in the village of Peniaban and were surprised to learn that tourists and visitors are welcome at these ceremonies. We were even invited to the luncheon banquet preceding the cremation procession. In the western world, death and grief are very private matters, but in Bali, it is normal to give a public farewell to the departed. The deceased woman had been almost a hundred years old, a distant but honored relative of the royal family. After the banquet, the body was placed in a gilded wooden replica of a pagoda and carried with pomp and circumstance to the cremation site on the grounds of the village's Vishnu temple. There was no prohibition on photography at any point in the procession or ceremony.

At the temple grounds, the woman's body was transferred from the pagoda to a giant wood and paper bull. After members of the family had made appropriate offerings, the butane burners were ignited and the bull was enveloped in flame. The Balinese believe that a person's soul will be released by cremation. Documenting this ceremony with our cameras provided us with a visual record of an insight into the culture of Bali and the religion of the people who accept death as the natural culmination of life.

Bali reveals itself like the native chambered nautilus shell, leading the visitor, step by step, into the innermost chamber. The traveling photographer must go beyond the resort and commercial areas to find the Bali we discovered, but the resulting pictures are well worth that effort.

PRINCE EDWARD ISLAND
Canada

PRINCE Edward Island is a summertime delight for a photographer. It certainly doesn't embody the cliché of the Canadian woods with bearded men wearing red plaid shirts and carrying hunting knives and deer rifles. Prince Edward Island proved to be an enclave of unexpected beauty. We found rolling farmland and neat, brightly painted houses with frequent sweeping vistas of the sea.

Not everything has a fresh coat of paint. We were intrigued by some of the old weather-beaten farmhouses, stripped of their paint by winter storms and salt air. We found one abandoned farmhouse on a bluff overlooking the sound, surrounded by a sea of goldenrod tossing in the wind. It looked like a painting by Andrew Wyeth. We wondered who had lived there, what their lives had been like, and where they had gone. The late afternoon sun etched the surface of the bleached wood and glistened on the glass of a broken pane.

We approached one farmer who was loading bales of hay onto a con-

veyor belt that carried them to the loft of his barn.

"Okay if we take a few pictures?"

"Yup," was the one-word reply. The Scots of Prince Edward Island are frugal with words.

During our visit we explored the ancient cemeteries populated by MacDonalds, Campbells, and Duncans. The tombstones spanned the generations. For some pictures we stretched flat on the grass, using a 24mm wide-angle lens to encompass both tombstones and church steeples in the background against the deep blue sky.

We watched fishermen returning from the sea, their holds laden with shining fish and lobsters. The creased faces of the fishermen were tanned by the wind and sun, affording us some excellent portraits. One evening we attended a lobster supper at the small village of New Glasgow. The bright red spiny crustaceans on our plates were so fresh they could have come from those same fishing boats. The claws were as big as our hands!

We were deeply impressed with the feeling of vast space, the fields of golden wheat, the expanse of the sea, and the blue void of the Canadian skies. It is sometimes difficult to capture this feeling on film, but we found one scene that did it for us. Driving along a coastal road not far from Charlottetown, we saw a lonely signpost at the edge of a wheat field. The weathered signs bore the names of farm families who lived nearby. A rutted road ran toward a blue strip of sea in the distance. We used a 24mm wide-angle lens set on infinity to record the stark beauty and loneliness of the scene.

Delvay-by-the-Sea is a lovely hotel that offers some fine picture opportunities with its unique architecture and spacious lobby. Originally the summer mansion of Alexander MacDonald, a former president of Standard Oil, this hotel is a reminder of a bygone era.

Charlottetown, the capital of Prince Edward Island, is not exactly a crowded metropolis, but it is a wonderful place for walking and recording the beauty of a quiet seaside town. We liked the old Victorian houses with the gingerbread porches and the flower boxes filled with red geraniums. We enjoyed taking photographs around the harbor late in the afternoon when the light sparkled on the water and illuminated the moored boats.

We came away from Prince Edward Island with a new awareness of the wide variety of geographic scenery that Canada has to offer the visiting photographer, ranging from the grandeur of the Canadian Rockies to these picturesque islands in the Maritime Provinces.

CHINA has five thousand years of history and a rich heritage of art and Buddhist culture. Much of this can be seen and appreciated in the temples and state museums but, for a photographer, the streets are China's great museums of life, accurately reflecting the culture, religion, and economy of the country.

The streets of China, however, haven't always been filled with excitement and vitality. During the reign of Mao Ze Dong they were devoid of activity. Farmers and craftsmen couldn't sell their own produce or products under the strict communist regime. In 1978, the new leadership allowed limited forms of free enterprise and the streets gradually came back to life. Today they teem with people selling and bartering food and merchandise.

On a recent visit to the bird and flower market in Kunming, an elderly painter and calligrapher caught our attention as he skillfully applied his brush to rice paper. The Chinese characters virtually danced on the white surface against the background of trees, water, and rugged mountains. We photographed him as he worked, while he glanced up at us and smiled from time to time. When he finished, he proudly held up his finished work and presented it to us. Our Chinese guide explained in English that the scroll read as follows: "Thanks for coming here and taking pictures of my painting. All the trees and mountains in my painting are happy and loving. China is a fair land with many scenic spots, and everywhere you can see talented men and women.

Now I am over seventy years old, but I still feel I have the strength to do more painting to make happiness for me and you."

This kind, gentle painter was typical of the people we met in China. They are friendly and open to tourists and usually don't mind being photographed. This gave us the opportunity to take many striking portraits. Most photographers are hesitant to walk up to strangers in China and ask

to take their pictures. We were delighted to discover that most Chinese are pleased to pose and are as interested in us as we are in them. They are especially pleased if you want to take pictures of their children. Since we don't speak Chinese, we used sign language or had our guide ask for us. We came home with an extensive portfolio of Chinese portraits.

Since the Chinese don't object to pictures, we took many candid shots on the streets and in the free markets of eastern and southern China. We found the 70–210mm zoom ideal for this type of shooting. Chinese markets abound with exotic and unusual images. Bamboo bird cages hang suspended in narrow alleys, their feathered tenants filling the air with sweet melodies. Fresh fruit and Chinese vegetables are piled high on the tables and carts of vendors. The colors are rich pigments straight from the palette of nature. The light in most Chinese markets is subdued and frequently very uneven. For most market shooting we used Kodachrome 200, but when there was enough light, we switched to Fujichrome 50. For some difficult shots we used fill flash with a slow shutter speed so that both the flash and existing light were recorded on the film.

North American travelers are not common in the western provincial city of Urumji, where we discovered elderly Uigher men with embroidered skull caps and flowing white beards sitting in front of their shops or stalls, sipping steaming cups of green tea. They regarded us with amusement as we took pictures of them with strange motor-driven cameras. White-capped young men

grilled miniature kabobs on skewers over glowing charcoal. We tasted these morsels of marinated lamb seasoned with coriander, cumin, garlic, and chilis, and they melted in our mouths, the spices stinging our lips.

We found countless little vignettes of life by strolling through Urumji's side streets and alleys. One of the most compelling scenes we found was in a beauty shop on Southgate Street. We stepped into the shop and were amazed to see a diminutive Chinese woman sitting under a massive curling machine that was a tangle of electric wires and lead weights. The weights applied pressure to each curl individually. Atop this Rube Goldberg device was a light bulb with a glowing red filament.

In Canton, we photographed the Pearl River and the sunset with two lenses, our 70–210mm zoom and 400mm telephoto, resting the latter on the concrete rail of our balcony. Freighters, ferries, barges, and sampans traced their way along the broad corridor of water, creating black silhouettes against the shimmering light of the setting sun.

Obviously, we love the streets of China. They offer many picture opportunities as well as the chance for adventure. Late one evening, for example, we left our hotel and spent several wonderful hours wandering through the crowds at the Beijing lantern festival. We once joined a badminton game on the street, only to be trounced by enthusiastic teenagers. The warmth and friendliness of the Chinese people cannot be measured. It is nice to travel and take pictures in a part of the world where Americans are made to feel so very welcome.

EAST AFRICA

DOING a self-assignment in East Africa is the ultimate photographic adventure. This part of the world has fired the imagination of zoologists, artists, and writers, including Ernest Hemingway, who immortalized "The Green Hills of Africa" with his battered portable typewriter and brought animal trophies back home with him. A few years ago, hunting and the sale of wild animal products, skins, and ivory was wisely outlawed in Kenya. Today the visitor can "bring them back alive" on film or videotape. We lead photographic safaris to Kenya and Tanzania each year, usually in August to coincide with the mass game migration from the Serengeti Plain to the Masai Mara. For many photographers, going on safari in East Africa is the fulfillment of a dream they have nurtured for years.

Starting with the basics, it is important to carry two camera bodies, and our advice is to have at least two zoom lenses, one ranging from about 28–90mm and the other from about 70–210mm. More advanced amateurs may also want a stronger telephoto, such as 300mm or 400mm lens, for certain game shots. Surprisingly, in many game preserves it is often possible for safari vehicles to get close enough to the animals to allow for good pictures with a normal lens.

We strongly recommend using transparency film as opposed to print film. The reason is simple. Color negative film makes it necessary to print every frame exposed to see the results, and this can be very expensive when one is taking hundreds or even thousands of pictures on a three-week trip. People on safari tend to overshoot, especially on game runs, since they never know when or if they will see a particular animal again. Be sure to take an adequate supply of film with you since, being imported, it is rather expensive in Africa.

Many visitors come to Kenya and Tanzania expecting to get interesting "people" pictures of the natives. Although this is possible, it isn't easy and in some places can even be dangerous. Most East Africans don't like to be photographed, especially members of the Masai tribe. Originally, their opposition was based on a superstitious fear of cameras, but in more recent years they have come to realize that

posing for a camera has a certain commercial value, and some will gladly pose for money. We strongly advise against taking any pictures of the Masai without their clear agreement.

There are certain basic restrictions that a photographer on safari in East Africa must accept. Most of the traveling and photography is done from a safari vehicle and with a driver/guide. The local guides have years of experience, know the parks, and can locate the animals. Don't drive through the game parks on your own with a rental car. It can be both dangerous and disappointing.

The first-time visitor to Africa should select a tour with an itinerary that includes the best photographic opportunities. Kenya and Tanzania are filled with game parks, lakes, recreational areas, and beaches of great beauty, but some are better than others for photography. We recommend:

The Masai Mara. This vast plain is host to a multitude of birds and animals living in a delicate ecological balance. You can stay in the comfort of luxurious tents at a site such as Governor's Camp or in the lodge at Keekerook. Park rules and the relatively smooth terrain allow vehicles to leave the road, permitting dramatic closeups of animals. In late July and August, hundreds of thousands of plains animals can be seen during the annual mass migration.

Mount Kenya Safari Club. This impressive lodge, set at the foot of Mount Kenya, is considered the most luxurious hotel in Africa. Ibis, crested cranes, pelicans, and marabou storks are only a few of the relatively tame birds you can photograph there closeup.

Amboseli. This preserve lies in the shade of Mount Kilimanjaro, the heart of Hemingway country, and has a wide range of animals as well as some special photographic problems. Much of the park has become a dust bowl, and the clouds of powdery dust can damage photographic equipment, so it is wise to protect it in plastic bags. Park rules don't allow vehicles to leave the road for closeup pictures of game. Everyone comes to Amboseli hoping to get a spectacular shot of elephants or giraffes against Kilimanjaro, but in our experience the snow-capped mountain is often shrouded in clouds and is only clear in the early morning or before sunset.

Ngorongoro Crater. Ngorongoro Crater, in Tanzania, is the world's largest caldera (collapsed volcanic crater) with unbroken walls. The interior measures 102 square miles. Features seen in the valley include rhinoceri, freshwater springs, forest, tree-lined streams, and Lake Mapadi, a highly alkaline lake occasionally visited by thousands of flamingos.

Lake Manyara. Tanzania's Lake Manyara is another wildlife refuge with the world's only tree-climbing lions. There is an abundance of elephant herds, birds, hippopotami, and wildebeest near the lake.

Mombosa. This very attractive beach resort offers a white sand beach in a tropical setting and an old Arab city with a lot of charm, but it has nothing in the way of animals. You can capture some compelling Winslow Homer-type images here.

Obviously, we have left out some very photogenic destinations in Kenya and Tanzania, but these are some of the highlights.

CHAPTER 1

Equipment and Film

A 70–210mm zoom lens can reach out and capture an image with a special spontaneity. This farmer in his rice paddy was photographed from a rural road on the island of Bali.

Photography is becoming more automated, and some professionals lament the loss of creative control with modern cameras. The functions of exposure and focus have been taken over by micro-chips and electronic circuits. Indeed, it is now possible to simply point and shoot with technically acceptable results. Contrary to some of our fellow pros, we believe that automatic exposure and autofocus make possible more spontaneous creative images. We feel it is far more important to concentrate on the subject than to get involved with shutter speeds, *f*-stops and critical focus. Events take place in a river of time, and the photographer must be alert and ready to record an image when it happens. Programmed exposure and autofocus allow us to catch those magic moments and preserve them on film.

Automatic and Autofocus Cameras

Automatic 35mm cameras fall into two broad categories: simple, relatively inexpensive cameras with one, non-interchangeable lens and the more sophisticated single-lens-reflex (SLR) cameras that can accept many different lenses. While the simple cameras can take fine-quality pictures, we will concern ourselves here with the newest autofocus SLR cameras. All of the cameras we will consider have the option of switching from automatic to manual control when the photographer wishes. There is little wonder that the consumer is bewildered by the complexity of this new technology. We purchased and tested the first two leading camera systems that went into autofocus seriously.

First on the scene was the Minolta Maxxum 7000, followed shortly by the more professional, but heavier, Minolta Maxxum 9000. Rising to the challenge, Nikon introduced the Nikon 2020. Olympus and Canon were not far behind in developing autofocus systems, and more brands enter the autofocus arena every few months. We wanted to try the autofocus cameras, and we chose to start with the two systems people usually look at for comparison, the Minoltas and the Nikons. Some of the attributes and drawbacks of a camera system are not apparent until you have tested the camera under field conditions. If you are thinking of buying an autofocus camera, perhaps the following observations will be helpful.

We liked the touch key controls and digital readout on the Minolta Maxxums and found them quick and efficient. Some photographers, however, may prefer the more traditional aperture and shutter speed controls on the Nikons.

The Maxxum 7000 and the Nikon 2020 are equals in many ways. They are approximately the same weight, and each has an efficient built-in motor drive and similar autofocus

systems. The Maxxum 7000 has an autowinder that takes thirty-six seconds, while the Nikon 2020 has a manual film rewind. If there is fast-changing action around you, thirty-six seconds can seem to be a very long time. On the other hand, if you usually take photographs of static scenes, the autowinder can be a convenience. Of the two, the Nikon tests best for professional or semi-professional use.

The Maxxum 9000 is our choice for heavy-duty professional use. The separate motor drive with re-chargeable nickel-cadmium (nicad) batteries is a decided advantage, but does add weight to the combined camera and motor drive. The option of spotmetering is a big plus.

The Nikon 2020 is a good bet for a person who already has a wide collection of Nikon lenses. The old lenses will not autofocus, but they do fit and interface with the camera; a green light shows in the view-finder when the lens is in focus.

For those of us whose eyes are not as good as they used to be, autofocus is not only an advantage; it is almost a necessity. How well does autofocusing actually work? Our tests show it works like a dream. There is a tiny rectangle in the center of the viewfinder which you place on the subject. As you press down on the shutter button, the lens focuses on the subject through power provided by a small ser-vomotor in the camera body. In focus-priority mode, a green light flashes in the viewfinder and the picture is taken. If you continue to press the shutter button, the motor drive will advance the film, the camera will refocus if the subject is moving and then shoot again. Fast moving subjects, such as sporting events sometimes cause a short time lag compared with a motor-drive

The 200mm zoom lens used for this picture, taken in Tampa, Florida, makes the moon appear relatively large. Stronger telephoto lenses will also enhance the size of the moon or the setting sun. Some photographers create very large moons and suns in their pictures by doing double ex-posures or sandwiching slides together.

film advance on a camera without autofocus.

Automatic exposure with these cameras can be achieved in the program mode or by selecting shut-ter priority or aperture priority. With these cameras, the photographer can pick the manual setting when desired. We believe that camera automation is an important tool for taking exciting photographs. It is important to remember, however, that images are created by the eye of the photographer and not by the technology of cameras.

At first glance the modern camera appears to be a maze of complex buttons and electronic controls which might very well drive some would-be photographers back to the simple point-and-shoot concept of the early box camera. In fact, most sophisticated 35mm SLR cameras include a mode for point-and-shoot operation, and many people use their cameras in this program mode. Certainly there is an advantage in being able to pick up your camera to point and shoot, knowing that the camera will focus and adjust ex-posure to provide a technically good picture. Such a mode is ideal for the photojournalist who must record images in fast-breaking situations.

Many amateurs have learned to use this program mode with their particular cameras but are uncertain about the alternative settings. We strongly recommend that a photog-rapher with a new camera read and study his or her instruction book carefully, but we do admit that some instruction books are difficult to understand and often omit impor-tant information. Different cameras and models have a variety of ex-posure modes, each of which has its own advantage. Some cameras, such as the Minolta Maxxums, have gone totally electronic with digital read-outs to show shutter speeds and apertures. This seems to be the trend in the photographic industry.

The alternative modes are usually "aperture priority," "shutter priority," and "manual." With aperture priority, you set the aperture, and the camera automatically sets the shutter speed. With shutter priority, you select the shutter speed, and the camera sets

the aperture. The former allows you to control depth-of-field to achieve selective focus, and the latter allows you to freeze action when necessary. These modes are chosen by an electronic or mechanical switch on top of the camera. The manual mode allows you to be completely free of the exposure system so that you can overexpose or underexpose as you wish.

Many new cameras are equipped with the autofocus features men-tioned at the beginning of this chapter. These focus the camera as you aim and press the shutter re-lease. It is important to remember that the small rectangle in the center of the viewfinder is the focusing target, and it must be on the subject which should be clearly defined. An autofocus camera will not focus on the clear sky or a blank wall. A switch on the camera will change from autofocus to manual. Many cameras are equipped with audible and/or visual signals to tell you if there is not enough light for a proper exposure or when the cam-era is in focus. It is our experience that autofocus cameras offer a real advantage to both the amateur and professional with quick and accurate focusing.

There is an ISO adjustment or setting on most cameras, although some brands and models set the ISO automatically when the film is loaded by means of a bar code on the film canister. When this feature is included and cannot be over-ridden, it is a disadvantage not to be able to readjust the ISO to your preferred level of exposure. (For instance, we usually set Kodachrome 64 on ISO 80.) We will discuss this in more detail in the film section. Most cameras also include plus and minus settings for exposure, which allows you to bracket your shots for slightly over- or underexposure. It is important to remember to return your exposure setting to normal after bracketing.

The AEL button on a camera is an exposure lock which allows you to take a closeup reading and then move back to recompose your pic-ture. This is especially helpful with backlit subjects. A few cameras such as Olympus and Minolta also have a switch for spotmetering, which can be very useful when you can't get close enough to a subject for a selective exposure reading.

Somewhere on your camera you will probably find a self-timer switch, a device that allows you to put your camera on a tripod and get into the picture yourself. Some self-timers are mechanical, but some are also electronic with a blinking light or audio signal. The light starts to blink after the timer has been activated, but it starts blinking much faster just before the shutter trips. Another use for the self-timer is to allow for short time exposures indoors without a tripod. We have placed the camera on the floor of a church to photograph the interior of the dome in dim light when the shutter speed is as slow as 1/2 sec.

Lenses

Many people purchase an SLR camera with a normal 50mm lens, and even though the camera is designed to accept a variety of different lenses, they live with the limitations of that one lens. Then they wonder why their pictures have a "sameness" about them.

As professional photographers, we find it necessary to use a wide range of lenses, and we have come to know what to expect from a telephoto, a wide angle, or a zoom. These additional lenses can add a new dimension of excitement to your photography. Many questions arise in picking extra lenses. What follows are some guidelines for selecting the best ones to meet your needs.

The 50mm or so-called normal lens usually has a relatively wide aperture such as $f/2$ or $f/1.4$, which makes it ideal for shooting under marginal light conditions. It is good for head-and-shoulder portraits and average scenes without a broad scope.

A wide-angle lens can be anywhere from 35mm down to 15mm. Wide angles tend to have a broad depth of field or sharp focus, meaning that under good light most elements in your picture will be in sharp focus. A wide-angle lens is usually associated with landscapes, but wide angles are often good for small groups of people and interiors. It is important to keep the camera level to avoid linear distortion in pictures of buildings and inside rooms, especially with the more extreme wide-angle lenses.

A telephoto lens ranges from 90mm on up to 1000mm, but any lens longer than 500mm is a highly specialized lens. On the lower end of the scale (90–135mm), a moderate telephoto works very well for close portraits. These lenses give a very pleasing perspective for pictures of a person's face. In specific scenes a telephoto tends to compress together such picture elements as traffic, crowds of people, or even fields and mountains in a landscape. This can be very interesting, visually.

Zoom lenses are designed to fill the needs of many different lenses of fixed focal length. For instance they can include a range of 28–90mm in one zoom lens and 70–210mm in another. This is very convenient for traveling photographers since it allows each to carry two lenses instead of five, but these lenses cannot compare in lens speed, or range of apertures with some of the fixed-focal-length lenses. For outdoor photography, however, they are ideal.

How do you choose a good second lens for your camera? Assuming that you already have the normal 50mm lens, your next purchase might be a 24mm or 28mm wide angle. Such a lens will be very useful for interiors and outdoor foreground/background compositions that use an object or person in the foreground and another compositional element in the background.

The next logical choice to add to your collection of lenses would be a zoom somewhere in the range of 70–210mm. This provides you the most useful telephoto focal lengths in one fairly compact zoom lens. It will enable you to stand in one fixed position while zooming in to crop and compose your picture. In the 200mm position this lens is ideal for picking out candid faces in a crowd.

A 400mm lens is a strong telephoto, and we have used ours for effective animal and bird pictures while on a camera safari in East Africa. With this telephoto, we have been able to get full-frame shots of exotic birds in the field and dramatic head shots of lions and cheetahs from the safari vehicle.

Most camera manufacturers will encourage you to buy their brand of lens to go with their cameras. Indeed, brand name lenses are of excellent quality, but don't hesitate to purchase your lenses from a good company that makes its own lenses to go on brand name cameras. These lenses are often less expensive and equal to the brand name lenses in performance. Some of the better-known makers of these lenses are Vivitar, Tamron, Tokina, Kiron and Sigma. Avoid unknown brands and bargain basement specials.

Open up the creative potential of your camera by selecting one or two additional lenses. Once you have enjoyed the advantage of a wide angle or a telephoto lens, you'll wonder how you ever got along without them.

Film

Regardless of where you go, film is the least expensive part of your trip, so be sure to have a good supply on hand. Your brand may not be available away from home, especially overseas. If you don't use all your film, you can freeze the unexposed rolls when you go home. This will keep it fresh, but it should be thoroughly thawed before exposure.

Some photo experts will hedge on the question of film, wanting to be fair and evenhanded, but any photo writer worth his salt should be willing to tell his readers what film he or she uses and why. When giving a photo seminar, we can always expect at least one person to ask what type of film we use. We shoot Kodachrome 64, Fujichrome 50, and Kodachrome 200 almost exclusively.

Basically, we consider Kodachrome 64 to be very close to a universal film. Technically, it is a color-transparency film, but top-quality color prints and even excel-

lent black-and-white prints can be made from the slides. (This is best done by a custom lab transferring the color slide to a black-and-white negative and making a print.) Kodachrome 64 is a dye emulsion film of moderate speed and is widely available throughout the world.

Fujichrome 50 is a grain-structure transparency film that has a tendency to exaggerate colors. This can be an advantage in some cases; for instance, on a rainy day it can spark colors. Greens and blues turn out very well on Fujichrome. More normal colors can be achieved by shooting Kodachrome 64. In poor-light situations we shoot Kodachrome 200. Kodachrome 200 is also daylight color-transparency film, but it has the advantage of having a higher film speed than Fujichrome 50 or Kodachrome 64.

The term "film speed" refers to

the film's sensitivity to light. This is most commonly measured and marked on film boxes as the ISO rating. The higher the number, the more sensitive a film is to light. Higher-speed films, such as Ektachrome or Fujichrome, are quite good, but they are grain-structure films and suffer to a slight degree in definition and sharpness in comparison to Kodachrome 25 and 64. The common film-speed ratings range from ISO 25 to 1600. In theory, and to some degree in practice, the slower film speeds will produce sharper pictures with less grain than their faster cousins.

There are two basic types of color film: color-transparency film and color-negative film. Walk into any camera store for a roll of color film, and the first question you are asked is "slides or prints?" If you're interested in prints, they sell you color-

We used a 400mm Nikkor lens to record this head of an ostrich in East Africa. To hold the lens steady we nested it on a bean bag on the roof of our safari vehicle. These giant birds often stand over ten feet high and run at high speed on their powerful legs. This one stopped for only a moment before turning to run.

negative film. That would seem to be logical, but you'll be shocked at how much it costs to have a jumbo print made from every frame on a thirty-six-exposure roll of Kodacolor film. If you're like us, you might only want two or three prints made from a single roll. With slides you can look at them in a hand viewer and pick the ones you really want. Having those few slides printed is less expensive than shooting color negative film and automatically getting prints of the whole roll.

We recommend using daylight color film for almost all picture-taking situations. Daylight color film can also be used for time exposures of a city at night and with electronic flash or strobe light. Tungsten-type color film works best under artificial studio lighting or those rare indoor situations where the only source of light is tungsten.

High-speed ISO 400 Ektachrome film allows you to shoot with a handheld camera in poor light. The quality can be good, but be prepared for grain and loss of defini-

tion compared to Kodachrome. It has been our experience that, over the space of ten or fifteen years, the developed Ektachrome slides are more likely to fade than Koda-chrome.

Kodak has come out with new VR-G color-negative film for prints with an ISO rating of 100. VR film is also available with ISOs of 200, 400, and 1000. (The last is the fastest Kodak color print film available on the market.) The quality of these films is excellent with good color fidelity and fine grain structure, but it is still costly to process and print every frame.

We have concentrated on Kodak film because it dominates the American market and is widely available throughout the world. There are, however, some exciting innovations by other film manufacturers. One of these notable developments is 3M's ISO 1000 color-transparency film which broke the film-speed barrier established by Kodak Ektachrome 400 for color slides. Kodak countered by coming out with Ekta-

Kodachrome 200 is a very sharp, dye-structure film. It is fast enough to catch images in marginal light, such as this portrait taken in a shaded street market in southern China.

Fujichrome 50 color-transparency film has the ability to enhance or exaggerate colors and is very effective for recording blues and greens. Notice the vivid quality of the sky and water in this picture of a young woman sunbathing on the beach in the Caribbean.

chrome P800/1600, a film that can be rated at ISO 800, 1600, or 3200. Kodak plants can only process this film at ISO 800 and 1600, but custom labs can push it to 3200.

Another interesting product is Polaroid's ISO 40 Polachrome CS transparency film. It can be developed in one minute with Polaroid's inexpensive new 35mm instant slide Autoprocessor System. The color quality is good, and the resulting slides can be mounted within minutes after the film is exposed.

Other film competition comes from abroad. Fujicolor and the Fujichrome, mentioned above, are from Japan and produce vivid and slightly exaggerated color images. These films are comparable to Kodak in cost. Fujichrome is still a relatively new film, so it is too soon to predict whether its slides will age any better than Ektachrome slides. Agfacolor and Agfachrome from Germany produce more muted color but are grainier than Kodachrome.

Regardless of the type of film we are shooting, we always rate the ISO on the camera at least one stop higher than the film's ISO. For example, we will shoot Kodachrome 64 at ISO 80 and Fujichrome 50 at ISO 64. This improves the color saturation, and we like the deep rich colors that result. You should shoot a test roll for each of your cameras. We have found, for example, that one of our cameras shoots the color saturation we prefer when the camera is rated two stops higher than the film ISO, while the rest of our cameras are rated at one stop higher.

Filters

Filters are a mystery to many photographers. The brochures for these little disks of colored glass and plastic promise spectacular results, but using a filter on your lens does not guarantee a better picture. Using filters requires talent, experience, and artistic judgment.

A filter is usually composed of plastic or optical glass and is inserted in front of the lens to alter color, color balance, or to change image geometry. Let us consider the merits of several basic filters for color film:

Clear glass filters. Photojournalists often use clear glass or skylight filters to protect the front elements of their lenses. (A skylight filter has a very slight warming effect on color film, but otherwise does not alter the image in any discernible way.) The ultra-violet (UV) filter, also relatively clear, has a minimal effect in eliminating aerial haze, but it is really not a very helpful tool in practical use other than protecting the lens.

Polarizing filters. The polarizing filter can be used effectively to eliminate reflections from the surface of water or glass. More important, it can darken a blue sky for dramatic impact. Care should be taken not to darken skies to ink-blue saturation.

Colored filters. Filters are available in a wide range of colors, but the most useful are blue, amber, and orange. Blue creates a desirable mood for some scenes, and orange imparts the warmth of the reflected light of the setting sun. Amber adds a gold tone.

Color balance filters. There are several important filters for changing color balance. The 85B filter converts Ektachrome tungsten film for daylight use. Special color-correction (CC) filters make it possible to use daylight film under fluorescent lights, and warming filters can add a desirable touch of life to an otherwise cold scene. Your photo dealer can help you select the precise type of correction to meet your needs, but remember that this is often a matter of individual taste.

As filters became more popular, various filter systems were developed to provide the creative photographer with a whole range of color correction, image alteration and special effects. One of these is the Cokin system which has a lavishly illustrated color brochure and guide. The Cokin and similar filter systems are based on the concept of a universal filter holder adaptable to all lenses through an adapter ring. These filters are square in shape and are held in place by a filter holder with a round, threaded adapter. The Cokin A-Series filter holder fits most 35mm cameras and lenses. Its P-Series is designed for large-format cameras.

In our opinion the Cokin graduated sunset filter is one of the most useful filters in our camera bags. This remarkable filter adds a touch of deep orange to the sky but changes the foreground color balance only slightly. The effect is pleasing and natural, particularly if you use this filter only in the early morning or late afternoon, when the light rays are slanted at a believable angle for a sunrise or sunset.

What other effects can be achieved with a creative filter system? There are too many to list here, but let us consider a few. For instance, a dream filter can diffuse highlights to create a soft, dreamlike effect. Such a filter, used with a small aperture, such as $f/16$ on the lens will create a double image, but opening the lens to a wider lens setting, such as $f/2.8$, will produce a much softer single image. A dream filter can be combined with a colored filter such as brown, blue, or sepia to create a mood.

Double exposure filters are also available, and we have seen some effective double-exposures that combine water and skylines to achieve a particular combination that may have existed only in the photographer's mind. This filter is half opaque and half clear and requires careful manipulation with your camera firmly attached to a solid tripod.

A star filter, more than any other, creates a sense of magic. It takes a bright reflection off glass, metal, or water and turns it into a bright star. It will do the same for lights of a city at night or even the highlight in a person's eye.

Electronic Flash Units

The avid travel photographer uses the sun as his primary source of illumination, but there are times when some form of supplementary

A Cokin graduated sunset filter gave this scene in Monument Valley a warmth associated with the late afternoon sun. Notice that the sky is darker near the top of the frame.

light is necessary to get the picture.

For a basic flash unit, the traveler will want a small, relatively lightweight flash head with rechargeable nicad batteries and automatic exposure. Popular units are Vivitar and Sunpak; of course, most major camera companies make their own brands. The recharging unit for the nicads should be adjustable to foreign current for travel abroad (110 volts should switch to 220 volts). An alternative is to carry a small Franzus transformer that switches 220 volts down to 110 volts. The principle is to recharge the batteries each night, but many pros also carry an extra set of charged nicad batteries as insurance. Too often, in-flash batteries become discharged accidentally when the switch is left on. We use a small piece of modeling clay to hold strobe switches in the off position.

Two basic types of autoexposure strobes are available. One is autoexposure with a light sensor on the strobe, the other is through-the-lens (TTL) autoexposure with a sensor at or near the film plane. The latter is more accurate, but both systems work extremely well.

One major problem with flash photography comes from having the flash unit mounted directly on the hot shoe of the camera. This usually results in a distracting shadow cast on the wall behind the subject, and the frontal light is almost always unflattering to people. Direct flash can also cause "pink eye" when the retina of the subject's eye reflects the light back into the camera. Fortunately these problems can be overcome by removing the flash from the hot shoe and using a connecting coil cord to hold the flash up and to one side of the subject. This high sidelighting is more flattering and interesting on a person's face.

With a tilt head or connecting cord it is possible to use the technique of bounce flash. This is when the flash is bounced off a white surface to illuminate the subject with a soft, even light. We have used bounce-cards effectively, but the most successful device for us is a plastic balloon called the Altrex flash

We photographed the two models with a sports car at night in front of the Caribe Hilton in San Juan, Puerto Rico. A multitude of tiny Christmas lights were in the shrubbery next to the hotel. The camera was on a tripod for a time exposure during which we fired two handheld flash units, swiveling the camera to get this unusual effect.

The two women playing the slot machines at Caesar's Palace in Las Vegas, Nevada, were illuminated by two flash heads with a 3:1 output ratio. The stronger light came from the right. Special permission is required to take pictures in any gambling casino.

This picture of Cleopatra at Caesar's Palace in Las Vegas, Nevada, was lit with two handheld flash units.

diffuser (check with your local camera dealer). Half of the balloon is transparent and half is opaque and white on the inside. When the balloon is inflated, the transparent side is attached with rubber straps to the flash head, and the flash is held off-the-camera and pointed away from the subject. We used the balloon with our Vivitar 283, but lost the automatic exposure function since the sensor on the flash was facing backwards. This was solved by purchasing a Vivitar accessory that allowed us to put the sensor unit on the hot shoe of the camera and connect it to the flash with a connecting cord.

Another option for creative lighting is multiple flash. We carry a total of three flash units with us, two of them fitted with accessory slave triggers. (All major brands have similar devices available.) These slaves are electric eyes that respond to the light from the master flash. It automatically triggers the other two units. Slave lights can be handheld by people, attached to portable light stands, or fixed in place by clamps.

TTL metering is available with dedicated flash and this provides precise exposure, metered directly from the film plane. There are several major brands, but the flash and the camera must be designed for use together. Multiple flash is also possible with the TTL system. TTL requires a connecting cord between the two flash units. Minolta has put out a Control Grip Set that provides all the necessary hardware and also makes possible a 3:1 lighting ratio. We used such a setup, for example, to light players at a casino in Las Vegas.

Bare-bulb flash is often used by professionals for effective lighting of room interiors, but most bare bulb units are expensive. Sto-Fen Products makes a useful plastic dome called the "Omni" that attaches to most portable electronic flash units and converts them to the equivalent of bare-bulb flash. Our tests indicated that autoexposure flash units will work with the Omni, but that light output is then reduced. It is necessary to run a test roll of color film with this accessory to insure proper exposure. Although not yet carried in camera stores, the Omni All Directional Bounce is available from Sto-Fen by writing P.O. Box G, Boulder Creek, CA, 95006. Be sure to specify the make and model of your electronic flash.

One of the most dramatic uses of flash can be achieved with the camera on a tripod to make a short nighttime exposure while illuminating people in the foreground. The subject could be a city at dusk with the building lights on when some ambient light is left in the sky. The

exposure for the city might be five seconds, just enough time to fire an autoexposure strobe with the open flash button to light the people in the foreground. It is wise to hold the strobe well off-camera to provide some modeling and underexpose with the flash by about one-half stop to simulate night conditions.

As travel photographers we always prefer to take pictures in bright, cheerful daylight, but it is comforting to have the knowledge and equipment which enable us to take pictures under any conditions.

Tripods

Most solid tripods are bulky, cumbersome, and awkward, especially for a traveler who has to carry them along with all of his other camera equipment and luggage. We have come up with some substitutes for a traditional tripod: bean bags, C-clamps, and table-top tripods.

The bean bag is a versatile and usually inexpensive accessory. On the roof of a car or on top of a fence post it can cradle a camera and hold it steady, even when you use a heavy long lens. The cheapest and fastest way to make a bean bag is to buy two pounds of beans in the supermarket and slip them into a zip-lock plastic bag, normally used for storing food in your refrigerator. Take that bag and insert it into another zip-lock bag with the top facing in and seal the second bag. This is the way we make our bean bags when on safari in Africa and find them to be highly satisfactory. You can also steal the bean bag from your child's toy chest or purchase a professional photographic bean bag known as "Steadybag," a product of Visual Departures in New York. It is expensive, but we have one and like it.

The next possibility is to use a C-clamp with a ball and socket tripod head. These are available at your local camera store and can be attached in many places. Our problem is finding a good place to attach it when we need it.

The third is to use a small, compact table-top tripod. Such a tripod can be carried in your camera bag and has small folding or telescoping legs which provide a steady base on a flat surface. Window sills, tables, and counter-tops work very well. It can even be pressed against a vertical surface such as a wall or a door jamb.

The Cullman Touring Kit is an interesting combination of accessories for the traveling photographer, including a C-clamp, suction cup, spike, and table-top tripod with a ball and socket tripod head.

When considering buying a "real" tripod, the three factors to consider are weight, size, and "steadiness." In the scale of tripods, there is one somewhere which will fit your

A tripod is an important accessory that enables you to compose under very controlled conditions.

needs. For 35mm SLR cameras, we like the Slik Universal U-212 Deluxe tripod. Closed, it is twenty-seven inches long and weighs about 5½ pounds, but we have found it to be rock steady, even in a strong wind. The telescoping legs will bring a camera to chest level on a six foot man and the elevator crank will bring it up to eye level. A tripod like this will meet most of your needs with most lenses and will fit inside a large suitcase. The Slik has a quick-release head that permits the convenient removal and replacement of the camera on the tripod. The best feature of the Slik is its instant-snap releases for the telescoping legs, which allows you to set-up on location in about thirty seconds. Other brands worth checking out are Gitzo, Bogen and Velbon. A tripod with a fluid head is essential for smooth panning with a video or movie camera.

Video

There is a revolution going on in vacation photography. More and more people carry video cameras to record their travel experiences in color, motion, and synchronized sound. The previously popular format of super 8mm home movies is quickly dying off in favor of video because it offers the user some unique advantages. Videotape is much less expensive than movie film and can be used over and over again. Millions of Americans now have television and VCRs, providing a quick and easy way to play back vacation tapes without having to set up a projector and screen in a darkened room.

Videotape is inexpensive, and one tape can provide up to two hours recording time. Exposure and synchronized sound recording is automatic. High-speed zoom lenses provide great visual flexibility. With all these advantages, there must be a fly in the ointment somewhere. Why doesn't every home-video buff produce prize winning shows? Most owners of video cameras shoot at random and playback their tapes exactly as they came out of the camera. Unfortunately, people rarely shoot scenes in the sequence that

would appear best on the screen.

The solution lies in the editing of home video. It can be done, but the equipment necessary for editing is rather expensive, and it takes considerable skill and time to do it well. Essentially, you need two VCR recording decks and a control unit, which allows you to take a scene from one tape and transfer it to a second tape. In addition, you need the equipment and ability to record and mix narration and music with the location sound that was recorded when the tape was being shot. This is all possible, but we should point out that approximately ninety percent of the owners of home video cameras don't bother.

The alternative is to plan carefully when shooting a tape. Write out a brief outline of your production, keeping in mind the purpose of your show. As an example, let's assume you're going to do a video-tape of your cruise vacation in the Caribbean. For a vacation trip, it is easy to videotape events as they happen. For instance, you'll want to show the departure from the dock when people throw streamers and confetti. Next, you may want to show people relaxing on the sundeck and around the pool. Plan to videotape each shore excursion at the ports where you stop, the people, the markets, and the beaches. Finally, you'll want to record the farewell party or the Captain's dinner. Shoot things in chronological order in short, meaningful "takes."

Some people fall into the trap of turning their camera on and letting it run, but when you're not planning to edit, such indiscriminate shooting is like making a boring speech that lasts for two hours. The goal is to have your final tape fast paced and lively. Remember that with shows produced "in-the-camera," you get what you shoot. Unlike movie film, you can't cut and splice the tape with scissors. After shooting an "in-camera" show, it is not difficult to record a narration on the separate sound track of the video tape with your VCR and a microphone, while viewing the tape. Using this "in-camera" approach will give you a very acceptable show without the

technical problems involved in electronic editing.

There are currently several basic formats in home video. These are Beta, VHS-C, and 8mm. VHS-C and 8mm are the most popular, but our tests show that the Super Beta format offers the best image quality. Self-contained video cameras now come with a built-in deck, and are very light and flexible.

Camera Bags

Many camera bags tend to be bulky and obvious. Not all of them are convenient for carrying the variety of equipment needed for a long trip. At least one of the bags we always carry is a Domke bag, designed by a professional photographer. These bags are rugged, natural, protective, and flexible, and have fold-over flaps, padded inserts, and velcro fasteners. The inside compartments can be modified easily to fit your particular cameras and lenses. Side pockets provide space for additional accessories. When we are facing an energetic photography walk, we often use the smaller Domke bags and belt pouches.

Another camera bag that impressed us was the Tamrac. The Tamrac 608 (Pro-system 8) is compact enough to fit under an airline seat or carry comfortably, but it is roomy enough for two camera bodies and several lenses. One main advantage we've found with the Tamrac camera bags is that they have a storm-tight zipper that, coupled with the usual velcro and snap-buckle closings, will protect your equipment in dust or bad weather. Another advantage is the design of the Tamrac shoulder straps, one of the most comfortable camera bag straps we've encountered yet.

Speaking of straps, Op/Tech has finally come to the rescue of both amateur and professional photographers who lug heavy cameras around their necks for hours on end. Op/Tech's 2½-inch-wide Pro Camera Strap is a soft stretch neoprene pad that makes a camera feel fifty percent lighter. We use the same type of Op/Tech Pro-Camera-Bag Strap for our carry-on luggage to alleviate the weight.

CHAPTER 2

Preparing to Go

Elliott Joseph, a member of one of our African camera safaris, is shown here shouldering a 400mm Nikkor lens for an early-morning game run on the Masai Mara. When planning a trip, it is important to decide which lenses will suit your needs.

To do in-depth coverage of a particular place takes a lot of advance planning, whether you're going to some exotic country or just taking a trip within the confines of North America. It is important to read or study about your destination before you go there so that you can plan what you want to photograph. Weather is an important factor on any photographic expedition, so be sure to avoid arriving during a rainy season, for instance. Clear skies and bright sun are usually the best conditions for taking pictures.

Having a car to carry you and your equipment to photographic sites is a distinct advantage and provides you with the mobility to explore. You may want to drive your own car from home, but if you're traveling a great distance, it may be more practical to rent a car after you arrive by air. Major cities in the United States and Europe have excellent public transportation. Driving a car in the city can be a liability because parking is difficult and getting around in urban traffic is a hazard.

If you rent a car, choose a light-colored model to help prevent your film from overheating when the car is parked in the sun and a trunk that locks so that you can store your camera gear. To make the most of your time, plan your driving so that photographic points of interest are within reasonable distances of each other. You may want to map out your itinerary in advance and mark photographic points of interest on a road map.

We always enjoy preparing to travel. Experience has taught us to check all the basics before we go. It would be difficult in the middle of the Gobi desert to find another zoom lens or more Kodachrome 64!

In addition to gathering and packing the right equipment, film, and clothing, sometimes there is a lot of official paperwork to wade through to obtain visas and passports. Immunization may be necessary for health certification. Even more fundamental, decisions have to be made about whether to travel alone, with a companion, or with a special photography tour.

Choosing a Photo Tour

Photographers are often disappointed by vacation tours not designed to meet their special needs. It is very frustrating for a photographer to be a captive on a tour bus which won't stop when a picture opportunity presents itself.

If you are not seeking instructions and photographic guidance, there are compelling reasons to plan your own itinerary and drive yourself. We often do this to shoot stock photography for our files. If you start from home, you can drive your own car. If you fly to your destination, there are some airline packages which will provide you with a rental car for a week at a reasonable price. With a

car you can stop whenever you please and explore back roads and villages at your own pace. Often you can schedule yourself to be at a site such as The Temple of Poseidon at sunset, which is far better than arriving at high noon when the architectural details are washed out from the overhead sun. With a car you can explore the countryside of France, the Swiss Alps, the Spanish coast, or the Scottish Highlands. Surprisingly, it is not difficult to drive in a foreign country.

The alternative is to take a photographic tour, one designed with photography in mind and composed of a group of people sharing an interest in taking pictures. Tours are designed with a carefully selected destination, a well-planned itinerary and a pace that allows time for adequate photographic coverage. On the photo tours we conduct, for example, we make an effort to be at the right place at the right time. This takes into consideration the light, the foreground, and often the activity at a specific location. Individual consultation should always be available for each participant on a camera tour, as each photographer, whether amateur or pro, is at his or her own level of expertise and has specific interests.

Try not to get into a crowded shooting situation. On our African safaris we try to limit each nine-person van to about six people; on other tours we use cruise ships, mini-buses, and even larger buses fitted with the amenities for ultimate comfort on the road. It is important that the drivers for a photo tour have been carefully selected to know and understand the needs of photographers.

In some countries a special effort is made to provide opportunities for people pictures in a friendly environment. At other destinations, the concentration is on wildlife and nature. In still others, the emphasis is on the culture and architecture of

Travel photography is a very individual, sometimes lonely art. Traveling alone can be avoided, but be careful to choose a group or companion with similar interests.

the region. The orientation should always be designed to give the participants the best possible picture–taking situation while providing basic information on the cultural and geographic aspects of the country or region. Our approach is to give our participants the opportunity to be personally involved in the activity which takes place at the destination. For instance, we cover the International Hot-Air Balloon Fiesta in Albuquerque, New Mexico and, if they wish, the tour members can arrange a balloon ride during the mass ascension of nearly six hundred colorful balloons. This is guaranteed to induce a Kodachrome frenzy in any dedicated photographer. Later, on that same trip, we provide Indian models at Monument Valley in Arizona.

In selecting a photographic tour, certain criteria should be kept in mind. The destination and itinerary are the two most important factors. Next you should consider the leaders and tour directors and their professional backgrounds. Are their credentials in photojournalism, museum-art photography, illustration, or stock photography? In short, can they teach you what you want to know? Beware of camera tours that don't list specific photo experts as leaders of the tours. The brochure may say "tours led by photo experts," but you may end up with a leader who knows the destination better than his cameras.

Some participants want to use their photography as a form of creative expression. Others may want to take pictures that can be sold to magazines through stock agencies and are interested in learning how to market their images to publications. Photo-tour operators will have brochures available, and these can tell you a lot about the qualifications of tour leaders, destinations and programs. In some cases you can expect formalized classroom situations, in-the-field film processing, and picture critiques by the leaders. Naturally, these tours are more academic and less mobile in nature than adventure tours to more exotic destinations.

If you're serious about photogra-

phy, a photo tour may be in your future. It is an interesting way to see the world and learn photography at the same time. A good place to look for tours geared to the needs of a photographer is in the back of photography magazines.

Traveling Alone

Some camera buffs don't want to travel alone, but can't find a traveling photographic workshop or tour to the destination they have chosen. Most of us would like companionship with a spouse, friend or at least a group with similar photographic interests. Quite aside from good company there are issues of personal safety, the safety of your photographic equipment, and the awkwardness of being a single. Most accommodations are priced by double occupancy with a hefty single supplement charged for people traveling alone.

The obvious solution is to join a group. Unfortunately, for photographers, unless you join a photo tour, you are too often forced to pass up compelling photographic opportunities because the bus won't stop or other members complain of the delay. Don't hesitate to seek out a compatible travel companion in the newsletter of your local camera club. It is advisable, however, to get to know your new friend before you set off together for a round-the-world tour.

Another solution is to subscribe to a service such as the Travel Companion Exchange, a computerized service that can put you in contact with other travel partners who want to share a prospective trip and who have similar interests, such as photography. Even if you don't actually share a room or cabin, you would still save money on a car rental and other such expenses. (For details of this particular service, you can write Jens Jurgen, Box 833, Amityville, N.Y. 11701.)

There are still other ways to solve the problems of being a photographer traveling alone. Hiring a guide can give you a companion who will know where to go to get the best pictures. Befriending a young couple will provide you with both

companions and models. The couple will obviously add interest to your pictures of places and provide scale to landscapes, monuments and buildings. Taxi drivers in foreign countries will often be willing to provide their services by the hour, but you should check with your hotel concierge as to whether the driver is both reliable and reasonable in price.

In some U.S. communities and in many foreign countries, there are hospitality groups. These were formed to show visitors the area's local sights and sometimes even take the visitor into local homes. An example of this is the Bahamahost program that offers a people-to-people encounter for any tourist who contacts the Ministry of Tourism in the Bahamas. This might include a sightseeing tour, a tennis game, a few friendly drinks or even a full dinner so that you can meet the friends of your Bahamian hosts. Using sensitivity and with the help of hour hosts, you'll usually come home with some incredible pictures of people and places. Often lasting friendships are formed and you'll find yourself returning the favor if your hosts visit your home town. Most of the foreign embassies or national tourist offices in the U.S. can give you information about whom to contact when you reach their country.

In the United States, you can usually get information on hospitality programs by writing to the "Convention and Visitor's Bureau" or "Tourist Information Board" of the state in which you will be traveling.

It would be a mistake to miss the trip of a lifetime because you do not want to be in a strange place without a travel companion. With some ingenuity, you can avoid being the lone photographer unless you specifically choose it for yourself.

A car can be a big help in getting those "unforgettable" pictures. We rented a car in Athens, Greece, so we could arrive at the Temple of Poseidon shortly before sunset. We were in position at just the right time to capture this spectacular sunset on film.

Paperwork

Don't forget your passport, health certificate, and airline ticket. If you have received hotel confirmation slips, be sure to take them with you. You should always carry half a dozen 2 × 2 inch passport photos in your wallet, but remember that in a few Communist countries, the photos must measure precisely 1½ × 1½ inches.

Several months before you leave on your trip, you should check with your county health department to see if you need immunizations. Often, you won't need any, but health authorities of various countries may require one or more of the following immunizations for entry into their country—polio, rabies, typhoid, cholera and/or yellow fever. To be valid, proof of immunization must be properly recorded and authenticated with an official seal by your county health department. If you need several immunizations, they must be properly spaced. Usually one month is mandatory between the time you are vaccinated with one live virus before you can be immunized with another. Some immunizations being taken for the first time are given in a series of three, with one month between each. With the exception of oral polio, and unless there is a substantial risk of infection, live virus vaccines are never given to pregnant women.

Your own doctor can prescribe malaria prophylactic medication, usually chloroquine, if there is a threat of malaria where you are going. In that case, you will need to start taking the weekly dosage about two weeks before your departure, and you should continue taking it until six weeks after your return.

At least one month before you leave (and earlier, if you are going to more than one foreign country), start working on your visa. Your travel agent will usually handle it for you for a fee. If you prefer handling it yourself, you can contact the country consulate, either in your city or in most gateway cities, to learn the proper procedures. Visas can be obtained by mail but the procedure is often quite slow.

This rural area in China is lovely, but it also poses health hazards for foreign travelers. Antimalarial precautions are a good idea here and elsewhere throughout rural Asia.

The State Department in Washington, D.C. has a travel advisory center, called the Citizens Emergency Center, that will send travel advisories to you free of charge if you are about to visit countries with uncertain security and safety conditions. You can call (202) 647-5225 to give them your address. No information will be given out over the telephone.

Organizing and Protecting Your Equipment

As professional travel photographers, we've learned to protect our cameras when we're on the road. Losing your camera or having it stolen can ruin an otherwise beautiful trip, but if you know how to protect your cameras and lenses there is very little chance of your being ripped off. In our case, we each carry at least two camera bodies and up to nine lenses, a virtual fortune in camera equipment. The same precautions we take, however, can be used by any traveler with a camera. These measures are simple and sometimes obvious, but it is surprising how easily a person having a good time on vacation can forget the obvious.

Before you leave home, put a name tag with your name, address and phone number on your camera strap and camera bag. Add the name of your hotel and room number in pencil after arriving at your destination. It is surprising how frequently people will go to considerable effort and trouble to return lost equipment if they know how to reach you.

We carry our cameras with us most of the time, and that includes taking them on the airplane in our soft shoulder bags to be placed under our seats or in the overhead compartment. There have been too many instances of lost, misdirected, or looted suitcases that have been checked through to a destination. That camera bag becomes as much a part of us as our right arms, and although we may walk around with one shoulder lower than the other, it is the one bag that we each carry up to the hotel room ourselves.

Actually one of the safest ways to carry your cameras is in a special jacket or a photojournalist vest such

CHECKLIST FOR THE CAMERA BAG

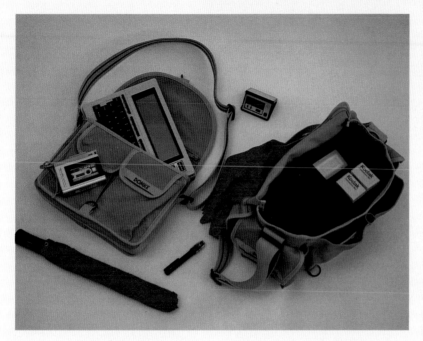

Most photographers take great pride in the camera bags they choose for packing all their equipment and accessories. We prefer soft-sided bags since they are expandable and conform to the body comfortably (see "Camera Bags" in chapter 1). Here is our checklist for packing our camera bags:

• Two camera bodies, a 24mm lens, a 28–85mm zoom lens, and a 70–210mm zoom go with each of us. We supplement these focal lengths with additional lenses to meet special needs. The extra camera body is crucial in case a camera malfunctions on the trip.

• We always carry an adequate supply of film with us on a trip. This is mostly comprised of daylight Kodachrome and Fujichrome and a few rolls of high-speed film (see the discussion about film in chapter 1).

• Large plastic zip-lock bags are a must for protecting cameras from rain, saltwater, or dust. They can also be filled with beans and used to steady the camera when you use telephoto lenses, and they are useful for carrying film through airport checkpoints.

• Plenty of spare batteries are mandatory. The most common cause of camera breakdowns on the road is weak or dead batteries.

• A cable release for time-exposure pictures and a compact electronic flash with a coil cord always go into our camera bags.

• Denatured alcohol, an old washcloth, and cotton swabs are useful for cleaning cameras. We decant the alcohol into an unbreakable plastic bottle with a secure screw cap to avoid leaks. Alcohol pads are also available in foil wrappers at your drug store.

• A small soft brush is the best tool for cleaning your lenses.

• A set of jeweler's screwdrivers can be used to tighten the very small screws that sometimes become loose from the vibrations of car and plane travel.

• A Swiss army knife with multiple tools can also be useful.

• A small pocket flashlight with fresh batteries will be needed for reading the camera controls in the dark when taking nighttime photos.

• Business cards, model releases, a spiral notebook, and pens.

• A medium-size folding tripod and/or a table tripod helps us take low-light or night-time photographs (see the discussion about tripods in chapter 1).

• Liquid lens cleaner and a good supply of lens tissue are necessities.

• Lens caps for the fronts and backs of all our lenses protect them on the road.

• Lens shades are helpful to prevent lens flare with backlighting and strong sidelighting.

• A portable automatic electronic flash goes into the side pocket of the camera bag with a slave attachment. Models with rechargeable batteries need an electrical convertor in countries that use 220 volts.

• A brightly colored kerchief or scarf and a red umbrella, windbreaker, or sweatshirt, preferably large enough so that it will fit on any cooperative model. Baggy is fashionable.

• A plastic rain bonnet folds to the size of a pen-knife and is large enough to cover your camera and lens in an unexpected downpour.

• A flat rubber disk (sold as a kitchen sink stopper) will help you unscrew lens filters if they are stuck.

• A roll of filament tape and a few strong rubber bands will often help you in an emergency. The rubber bands can be used to seal the package if you put a camera into a plastic bag for protection.

• We always carry a small canvas wallet to hold our filters. Our favorite three filters are the graduated sunset filter, polarizing filter, and clear glass. The last is used for protecting the optical surfaces of our lenses.

• Put instruction books for cameras and flash in a side pocket of your camera bag.

We often carry a red umbrella as a colorful prop. In Salvador, Brazil, it came in handy for this unusual shot of two models posed in front of a wall painting.

as those described on page 66. These unique garments literally serve as a camera bag with a multitude of special pockets and compartments. Cameras, lenses, film, and accessories fit neatly into the pockets, and it is unlikely that photographers would walk away from a garment they are wearing.

It is not smart to walk through the lobby of a hotel with one or more expensive cameras hanging around your neck. It doesn't pay to advertise yourself as a walking camera store. Put your cameras in your shoulder bag except when you are shooting. We carry our equipment in bags which are not the leather or metal cases traditionally associated with cameras. The bags we use are canvas, dirty, and a bit threadbare around the edges. The worst kind of bag is expensive leather with the brand name of Nikon or Canon emblazoned on the outside. That is virtually an invitation to have someone make an unauthorized visit to your room while you're not there.

Some professional photographers carry their cameras in metal aluminum cases with combination locks and use bicycle chains looped through the handle and the bathroom sink pipe or bed frame with a separate lock for the chain. This is both formidable and impressive, but to a potential thief the message is very clear: "This metal case contains something worth a lot of money." A crowbar will easily break off the handle of the metal case in three seconds.

The luggage we take on trips is hard sided with combination locks. When we check into a hotel, we unpack our clothes, put them away and then put our camera bags into the luggage and lock it. This is certainly not a foolproof procedure, but at least the cameras cannot be seen. When we go out for any reason without our cameras, we put a "do not disturb" sign on the door and turn on the television set at a moderate volume. We can't guarantee the safety of your cameras if you take these precautions, but in over four-million miles of travel as pro-

fessional photographers, we haven't yet had a camera stolen.

The next concern is a direct theft by the "grab and run" method or by armed robbery. In the first instance, don't make yourself an easy mark by carrying your camera casually over one shoulder. Put the camera strap around your neck and, whenever possible, don't walk alone in a strange city or a questionable neighborhood. Mountain Adventure puts out a camera harness/strap that was originally designed for hikers. Not only will it relieve pressure on your neck, but it makes camera snatching more difficult. (Although this is not available at all camera stores, you can write 2915 Estrella Brilliante N.W., Albuquerque, N.M. 87120.)

Undoubtedly the most distressing way to lose your camera is at the point of a gun. If a thief threatens

In Shanghai, China, there is almost no crime or theft on the crowded streets. Unfortunately, the same cannot be said for American cities, where you should always be careful of your camera equipment.

involved in the picture-taking process, but it is vitally important not to put the camera bag down and wander off in a quest of those unforgettable travel pictures. Stick to that camera bag like glue, and if you must put it on the ground to take a picture, put your foot through the carrying strap. The only time to leave your camera bag is when you have a trusted friend to watch it.

It is never wise to leave your camera equipment in your parked car, but above all don't leave it on the back seat or in a hatchback where it can be seen. This is virtually an invitation for someone to smash the window and help himself. If you must leave your camera in your car, put it in a locked trunk and take care that you are not observed placing it there. Please remember, however, not to put your camera or film in a car trunk during extremely hot weather.

Guarding Film from X-Rays

As security measures at airports increase, there has been understandable concern on the part of traveling photographers about the effect of x-rays on exposed and unexposed film at airport security check points. Light-sensitive film can be fogged by x-rays, but this fact is often a matter of degree. The actual level of damage results from a combination of several factors. These are the ISO rating or light sensitivity of the film, the strength of the x-ray, and the accumulation or number of times the film has been exposed. It has been shown that x-rays have an accumulative effect on film.

In practical terms, this means that slow-speed color films, such as ISO 25 or 64 daylight film, can be passed through a normal x-ray machine in an American airport once or twice without danger of damage. It becomes a grey area with potentially grey pictures if the film passes through more than one security checkpoint in spite of the disclaimers on the x-ray machines stating that they will not damage film. High-speed film is at greater risk and requires greater precautions.

Federal Aviation Authority regulations specify that items will be hand

you with a gun or physical violence, don't argue. Hand over your camera and count yourself fortunate to escape with your life. If your camera is stolen, immediately report the loss to the police and keep a copy of the report for your insurance company.

You may want to investigate camera insurance. We carry a floater on our homeowner's insurance policy to cover theft, loss, or damage of our professional equipment. Rates vary with different insurance companies and you can cover other items besides cameras on the same floater policy. It is a moderate investment for extra peace of mind.

All of us tend to get deeply

checked, if requested, at American airports. This is reassuring to serious photographers, but there are things you can do in advance to make sure that such a hand check is quick and painless. Our advice is to take all of your film out of the yellow boxes and plastic cannisters and place it in a clear vinyl bag. We use the heavy zip-lock bags from our kitchen. This can be carried in a compartment of your camera bag or in any carry-on shoulder bag. The film can be pulled out quickly for hand inspection at the checkpoint. If you leave the film in the plastic cannisters, the inspector must open each and every one. Understandably, he or she will balk if you are carrying many rolls of film and a long line of impatient passengers is standing behind you.

Because some inspectors may be new on the job and not knowledgeable about the potential damage to high speed film, they may be tempted to take the plastic bag out of your hand and put it through the x-ray machine. It is better, therefore, if you actually open the bag and hold it so that they can look down at the film while you explain why it is so important not to x-ray the film. Be courteous and patient and, above all, arrive early enough for your flight so that neither you nor the inspector is in a hurry.

There is no guarantee that film will be hand inspected, especially overseas, but the traveler should be appreciative of security measures. These precautions are taken to prevent terrorism and save lives. The life saved may be your own. At peak travel periods and times of airport congestion, security guards may not have the time to hand inspect your film. Remember a one-time exposure probably won't harm your film if the ISO is less than 1000.

Security procedures vary from country to country. Currently France, Denmark, Belgium, allow no hand inspection. In London, we were recently advised that the new security rules will call for all film, without exception, to go through the x-ray machine. In such places, you may wish to put your film through the x-ray machine in lead-shield bags

PROBLEM SOLVING ON THE ROAD

Problem	Solution
1. Camera malfunction	Check camera batteries. Ninety percent of camera problems are due to the batteries. Be sure to carry spares. Check your camera manual for other possible solutions. Find a repair shop. We carry an extra camera body for backup.
2. Out of film	The best way to avoid this is to take more than enough with you. In the U.S., Europe, and Japan you can find film in most major cities. Check dates for freshness.
3. Broken eyeglasses	Losing or breaking your eyeglasses can put you out of business for taking pictures. It is advisable to carry an extra pair of spectacles with you. If not, you can pick up a pair of usable reading glasses in a drugstore. Remember that autofocus cameras allow you to shoot without focusing.
4. Dirty cameras	Carry lens tissue, lens cleaner, cotton swabs, and foil-wrapped alcohol pads to clean dirt, grime, and salt spray from your cameras and lenses. You can protect your cameras by keeping them wrapped in plastic bags, even when packed in your camera bag or case.
5. Lost cameras	The best way to avoid loss or theft of cameras is to keep them with you at all times. Don't walk away from a camera bag, even for a moment. If you do lose your cameras, replace them at a photography shop in the nearest city. Purchase your known brand if possible. If your cameras are stolen, file a police report for insurance claims. Be sure to have a list of model and serial numbers in your suitcase.
6. No tripod	Brace your camera against a hard, flat surface, vertical or horizontal, to make a time exposure at night or in dim light. A good tripod substitute is a bean bag. It can be made on-the-spot from beans and a plastic bag.
7. Flash failure	Check batteries and connecting cords or hot shoe contacts. If this doesn't correct the problem, switch to a high-speed film and a fast lens and shoot with existing light.
8. Fogging lenses	Lenses will sometimes fog up when stepping out of an air-conditioned hotel to a hot and humid environment. Don't wipe. Wait about ten minutes for the lens to clear naturally.
9. Film pulled out of the cartridge while in the camera	If film comes off the spool in camera, open the camera body in a completely dark room, such as a hotel closet, and put the exposed film in an opaque film canister. Label it for the film lab with a warning, and deliver it for processing. If you're outdoors, borrow a thick jacket, put your arms through the sleeves backward, and turn it inside out to form a portable darkroom.

The airstrip on the Masai Mara plain in Kenya doesn't have x-ray machines for security checks, but most airports do. To avoid x-ray damage to your film, we suggest you always request a hand check for it.

manufactured by the Sima Corporation. Each bag will hold a twenty-roll pack of 35mm film. Extra-heavy lead foil bags are available for high-speed film.

X-rays won't have a detrimental effect on video recording tape or audio tapes, but the strong magnetic field in the walk-through metal detectors can cause problems with these materials. If you can, ask for a hand inspection.

Most checked luggage is not x-rayed, but if you do pack film in your suitcases, we suggest using the heavy duty Sima lead-shield bags. When x-rays are used on locked luggage, the dose is much stronger than the type used for hand luggage.

Taking the Right Personal Gear

Most photographers like to dress so that they can be identified as pho-

tographers. Serious amateurs and professionals join their fraternity by choosing the right hat, jacket, or vest. Obviously, clothes don't help a photographer take better pictures, but the right choices can provide comfort when you are on assignment. Deep pockets for instance can accommodate film, lenses and accessories. Indiana Jones may be a romantic character as he fights off villains in the Temple of Doom, but his felt hat and battered leather jacket are not really practical for the travel photographer. We like cotton for warm weather and a water repellent jacket over layered sweaters for cold weather. An insulated parka is necessary for the Arctic.

We have tested and used a number of jackets, vests, and bags on our assignments. Banana Republic carries a fine line of cotton traveling clothes. Their bush vest can be used as a photography vest and fits neatly against the body. Their photojournalist's vest has twenty-two convenient pockets. If you don't mind a bulky look, Bazooby has also come out with a photo vest that serves as a portable camera bag. It has twenty-two pockets, six of them foam padded, and has front velcro tabs to hold your camera close to your body.

We personally prefer a more streamlined look and found this in the Domke jacket. It provides ten deep pockets but doesn't look lumpy when not stuffed with photo gear. For warmer weather, we like the new sleek Domke vest. Velcro fasteners in all of the Domke clothing give you easy access to equipment carried in pockets.

We've been impressed with several brands of cool, lightweight cotton canvas shoes, but for all-around city hiking and evening wear, we prefer a leather hiking shoe which looks good enough to wear with a jacket and tie after we've finished our sunset shots. When it turns cold, we've found that Isotoner gloves allow us the flexibility we need for taking photographs without removing our gloves. Finally, many hat shops can provide you with a felt Indiana Jones hat, but we've found a cheaper and cooler cotton version of the same hat at Sears & Roebuck.

Packing Your Suitcase

Packing for a photo vacation is an art in itself. Obviously, you need much more than a swim suit and suntan oil. What you take and how you pack it can make a big difference in the quality of the pictures you bring back.

At least two weeks before you leave on your trip, you must make crucial decisions about camera equipment, film and clothing, while you can still purchase those items you don't have. You should have already obtained your visas and had the necessary immunizations. Now it

is time to pack within the trip's strict limitations of space and weight.

You should pack at least a full day before your departure and use your check lists for equipment, film, accessories, and clothing. Probably part of your photographic gear will be packed in your suitcase. Pack your hard items and accessories in among soft items, using sweaters, skirts and slacks to cushion them against impact. Putting your folded clothing in large zip-lock bags will prevent creasing.

Heavier items should be at the back of the suitcase so that they will be on the bottom when the suitcase is in an upright position. Liquids in plastic bottles should be put in plastic zip-lock bags to protect your clothes and equipment against spillage or leaking. Most compact tripods will fit diagonally across the bottom of a suitcase, but you might find it expedient to take your tripod with you when buying a suitcase. For some vacation destinations, you may need an extra suitcase.

On a long trip you will be carrying great quantities of film, and it may not be possible to fit all your camera equipment and film into your camera bag. The rule we follow is to personally carry our equipment on the way to our destination. If our luggage should be lost, we could buy film but wouldn't need to shop for cameras. Conversely, on the way home, we carry our exposed film in our camera bag and pack our equipment in the suitcase if necessary. If the luggage were lost, the equipment could be replaced, but our exposed film could not be.

Having packed, you can now relax. We like to pack a day or two early so that last minute items can be tucked into the corners of our suitcase. We want to make our departure day as care free as possible. After all, we are on our way to indulge ourselves in our favorite pastime; seeing new places and taking exciting pictures.

EMERGENCY KIT

Depending on where you're going, you may want to take some basic first-aid and health-care items along with you. In certain parts of the world, it pays to be prepared in case of an emergency. You should, of course, check with your doctor to be sure that any medication you bring is safe for you to take. You might want to pack:

- An extra pair of prescription glasses or contact lenses if you wear them

- A thermometer

- Bandaids

- Bactine or sterile cleanser and antibacterial ointment for burns, cuts, and minor abrasions

- Foot powder or fungus ointment

- Pepto-Bismol pills

- Motion-sickness pills or patches if you need them

- Kaopectate for diarrhea

- Sore-throat or cough medicine

- Dry-skin lotion

- Insect repellent

- Sunscreen preparations

- Ace bandages, antacids, and water-purification tablets

CHAPTER 3

Photographing Cities

The tile roofs and wooden beams of these buildings in Copenhagen make this photograph a study in graphic design, and they also identify the Scandinavian architecture unique to this charming city.

Wherever you travel, you will find a rich variety of stimulating images to capture on film. Discovering the visual drama of man-made cities is the traveling photographer's business. When you get to a town or city, the concierge at your hotel or the local tourist bureau can supplement your preliminary research. Most tourist bureaus publish a visitors' guide that includes color photographs and walking tours of cities. Local inhabitants can often tell you the best vantage points for photographing the sunset on the canyon rim or for framing a good picture of a city's skyline. Take the time to ask questions and get advice before you start out to take pictures. After you explain what types of subjects you want, you'll find that local people are eager to help. They may direct you to the farmer's produce market or to a local event such as a fair or rodeo taking place that day.

When you're photographing a city, start exploring early in the day, and pay attention to the way the city comes to life. Look for visual cameos to record with your camera. Since it's difficult to shoot at high noon, the middle of the day is a good time to locate good vantage points for shooting in the late afternoon when pictures benefit from the warmer, low-angle light. Later on, position yourself for dramatic sunset shots with a telephoto lens by scouting for the best locations earlier in the day.

If you've never been to a city before, take a sightseeing tour to get an overview and determine where the best pictures can be found. Although there are opportunities to use your camera on some tours, you'll probably find it more useful to jot down addresses and locations for a return visit. For example, observing the position of the morning sun on a building, you can use your compass to determine where and when the sun will set, or you can note what time the farmer's market opens and where the city parks are located. Cities that are compact, such as San Francisco and Seattle, and those with good transportation systems, such as London, are easier to cover without a car than spread-out cities such as Los Angeles.

The cardinal rules for photographing any city are to travel light, to wear appropriate clothes for the weather and climate, and most of all, to wear comfortable shoes with arch-supports or walking shoes with crepe soles. Carry your equipment in soft canvas cases with velcro flaps and convenient compartments for lenses and film, and put everything else in your photography vest or jacket, distributing your gear so that its weight doesn't fall directly on your neck.

Generally, limit your equipment to one 35mm camera body, one very wide-angle lens such as a 24mm, one 28–85mm zoom, one

Postcards and tourists' snapshots are filled with such travel-photography clichés as the United States Capitol and the most photographed lady in New York. We shoot clichés for our stock files since some art directors and publishers seem to thrive on them, but we also try to shoot the same subjects from more creative points of view.

70–210mm zoom, and a high-speed 50mm lens for available-light interior shots. Take plenty of daylight film—a minimum of ten rolls per day—and carry a few extra rolls of high-speed film for low-light situations.

A few additional items are helpful to have along. A red umbrella or colorful windbreaker comes in handy during bad weather in more than the obvious ways. If the day suddenly turns cloudy and you are trying to photograph a drab gray structure, a spot of red can make the picture come alive. Also, a small tabletop tripod can be invaluable. If you're traveling by car, bring a larger tripod to use after dark and in low-light situations.

Look for subjects that symbolize your location and make it distinctive. For example, when covering Washington D.C., be sure to get some good shots of the Capitol Building, and when you are in New York City, shoot the Statue of Liberty. Some people might consider these subjects too cliché, but they don't have to be. A cliché results from shooting an ordinary subject in an ordinary way. Strive to bring a fresh perspective to everything you see in the viewfinder. Find unusual vantage points and try a variety of focal lengths on your subject. With a little extra effort you are much more likely to bring home memorable pictures.

When traveling in foreign cities, search for scenes that reflect the culture of that particular country. You may find such images in regional architecture, art, people, or even on your dinner table. A bottle of wine next to a loaf of French bread clearly says the picture was taken in France. A red double-decker bus is an equally powerful symbol of London.

Cities are composed of and by people, and to be accurate and comprehensive any urban travel coverage should include pictures of people at work and at play. If you approach people with a smile, they will usually be willing to pose for you (see "Focusing on People" in chapter 4).

Another facet of a city is its reflections. Many skyscrapers and modern buildings have glass walls. Windows that are reflective mirrors are useful for taking unusual pictures of pedestrians, traffic, night lights, and other buildings. Some of the resulting pictures will be abstract patterns; others will be skewed versions of reality. Photographing reflections is a good way to depict architectural contrasts: for example, an old fashioned Victorian building mirrored in the stark glass wall of a skyscraper.

Sculpture, statues, fountains, and store displays are also compelling urban subjects waiting for your creative touch with a camera. A statue of a dignified general pointing toward battle front will look a little more human with a pigeon sitting on his finger. A rainbow of light glowing in a fountain's water spray is often visible if you position your camera correctly. Shooting sunlight through spraying water is visually very effective. If you use a fast shutter speed, each water drop becomes a frozen diamond.

Posters, signs, and graffiti are also good subjects for photography. For example, in London we once came across a wall scrawled with the words: "PRUNES, PRUNES, EAT YOUR PRUNES!" Signs can be humorous, make political statements, or even suggest clever puns. Keep your eyes peeled for any verbal artifact that might make a good picture. Store windows are a good source of unintentionally humorous scenes. Use a polarizing filter to eliminate daylight reflections in the glass.

Giving yourself enough time is an essential element in taking good travel pictures. To do justice to Beijing, China in two hours, for example, is impossible, although you can drive through the city in sixty minutes. Under ideal circumstances a full week of shooting would start at sunrise and continue through sunset. This would allow adequate time to photograph the city's streets, monuments, and people under a variety of lighting conditions.

Finally, try to photograph the city's

Be on the lookout for pictures that have a touch of humor. This London shop window, filled with discreetly draped mannequins, makes a statement about British modesty.

Photographing store signs, such as a hotel's advertisements in India (top right), helps the viewer identify and perhaps learn more about what a city has to offer.

The spray from this fountain in St. Louis (bottom right) was frozen by a fast shutter speed into thousands of tiny ice crystals. Backlighting created a strong, monotone image with an almost surrealistic quality.

A spot of color adds visual interest to a picture taken on a rainy day. The red wheels on this horse carriage in St. Peter's Square in Rome show the difference a primary color can make in an otherwise drab scene.

We were up early in the morning to capture Manhattan's golden skyline (top left) along Central Park West. Light has a special warm and vibrant quality early in the morning or late in the afternoon. No matter where you are, you'll get your most dramatic pictures just after sunrise or during the two hours before sunset.

This shot of New York City (bottom left) was taken from the top of the Empire State Building. We waited until the sky was clear and went to the observation platform shortly before sunset with our camera on a tripod. As it began to get dark, the lights of the city started to come on, which turned the dark buildings into honeycombs of light.

skyline. Ask for directions to find the best vantage point. The very best view will highlight several distinctive landmarks that clearly identify the city. Shooting a skyline at sunrise or sunset is preferable because of the dramatic lighting and color.

Photography can be challenging and lots of fun as you try to capture the distinctive character and personality of different places on film. This may entail searching for an evocative mood, unique architecture, or a collage composed of vibrant colors or people's faces. If you arrive with a good supply of film, boundless energy, and a creative eye, you'll always return home with a fine collection of photographic memories.

Architecture

Architecture often inspires a sense of awe which springs from the

awareness that you're looking at herculean efforts of creative genius. Ancient buildings designed and created by men may have taken generations to construct, but you have the opportunity to record them with your camera in a split second. There are a wide variety of architectural styles. Europe provides a virtual feast of architecture, ranging from Greco-Roman ruins to the Bauhaus School's chrome and glass innovations. The gothic flying buttresses of Notre Dame, the frothy embellishments of a rococo church in Bavaria, and the classic beauty of the Parthenon atop the Acropolis are all exciting photographic subjects, but often photographers can't capture on film the beauty and grace they see and appreciate with their eyes.

Although photographing architecture successfully takes patience and the right equipment, you don't have

This composition of the church in the Taos Pueblo in New Mexico makes effective use of the graphic design elements in adobe construction. We enhanced the blue sky by using a polarizing filter to make the white crosses stand out.

Linear distortion in the vertical lines of buildings can work to your advantage. We shot this skyscraper in San Francisco with a 24mm wide-angle lens. The converging lines draw the eye to the top of the frame.

to be a technically skilled architectural photographer tilting and elevating a view camera on a tripod to correct the divergent lines of an errant building. Travel photographers can employ a much less complex approach by using a simple 35mm camera with through-the-lens (TTL) focusing and still produce highly professional architectural pictures that could grace the pages of as prestigious a publication as *Architectural Digest*.

There are some basic rules about photographing linear structures, and although the rules can be broken, understanding them is the first step toward improving your pictures of buildings. Tilting your camera upward to include the top of a building creates linear distortion, which translates as a feeling that the building is leaning backward in the picture. Linear distortion can be avoided by keeping your camera perfectly level so that its film plane is parallel to the building's vertical surface, but this often cuts off the top of the structure. If you break the rule about keeping the camera level, and many people do, you must be willing to accept the distortion. The solution to the problem is to use a perspective-correction (PC) lens. Putting a PC lens on your camera lets you elevate the front element of the lens and thereby include the top of the building while the camera stays level. This simplified form of the view camera allows photographers with 35mm SLR cameras to do serious architectural photography.

The tripod is another important tool for photographing buildings. Most travelers want one that is solid, lightweight, and compact. Slik makes a model that fits into a large suitcase. Be sure that whatever tripod you purchase has rubber tips for a firm protective footing. Tripods are necessary to prevent camera movement when working outdoors at night or around dusk. Under these lighting conditions, exposures should be made with a cable release. One of the other major advantages of a tripod is to provide solid support for taking interior architectural shots in dim light.

Photographing Interiors

Interior pictures are best done with a wide-angle lens since a wider angle of view enhances the feeling of space and shows more of what the eye encompasses. People often don't realize the limited scope of a normal 50mm lens until they use it to photograph a room and produce a picture showing one uninspiring corner. A 24mm or 28mm lens is wide enough to give a real feeling of what the room looks like, which is, after all, the goal of architectural photography.

Unfortunately, most travelers with cameras don't even try to record the interiors of great churches, interesting buildings, and cozy pubs because they assume the technical problems of flash, tripods, and time exposure are too great to overcome. Well, that is seldom the case. First of all, there is more natural light inside buildings than most people realize. For example, when you step inside a cathedral from bright outdoor sunlight, the church initially appears very dark. As you let your eyes adjust and look around, you may notice that light is coming through stained glass windows and clerestory windows in the dome and that artificial light and maybe even candlelight illuminates the altar. Many photographers don't realize that a camera is capable of accumulating this light and recording it on film during a time exposure. Daylight color film is the best type of film for working with such diverse sources of light, rendering results in lively, warm tones that are pleasing to the eye.

Time exposures should be made on a tripod with a cable release and really aren't complicated if you fol-

This pub scene in Ireland was also part of our assignment for the Irish Tourist Board. We shot it with a 28mm wide-angle lens on Kodachrome 64, using a combination of window light from the left and tungsten light from the fixture over the bar on the right. Notice that the barmaid is in sharp focus and the background is slightly out of focus, which helps to concentrate your attention on the subject. We achieved this by shooting at the widest aperture.

Using a solid tripod helps deliver needle-sharp pictures in marginal light, but there are some places where tripods aren't allowed. We made this picture of the statue of Thomas Jefferson by mounting our camera on a tabletop tripod and bracing it against one of the marble columns in the Jefferson Memorial. The exposure was 1/2 sec. at f/8 on Kodachrome 64.

low a few simple rules: 1) Use a relatively wide angle lens (28mm or wider). 2) Keep the camera as level as possible. 3) Make sure the tripod is solid and the camera is securely attached. Set the aperture at about f/5.6. Shooting with a wider aperture won't provide adequate depth of field. When the camera is used in an aperture-priority mode, the automatically selected shutter speed will vary according to the lighting conditions—it could be as slow as one or two seconds with color film. You will be surprised how well these interior pictures will turn out.

In buildings where using a standard tripod is forbidden, you are often permitted to use a table-top tripod. It can be placed on the floor or braced against a wall or doorway frame. Without a tripod, the camera itself can be braced against a solid surface for exposures of one second

or less, or you can shoot up at the ceiling or dome of a church with a wide-angle lens by putting the camera flat on the floor and activating the self-timer.

Using high-speed daylight color-transparency film is another solution for interior shots where tripods can't be used. In such situations Ektachrome 400 or even ultra-high-speed Ektachrome P800/1600, a film that can be pushed as high as ISO 3200 in processing, are good choices. Even in almost nonexistent light situations, you can still easily handhold the camera at 1/30 or 1/60 sec. by rating the film at ISO 1600. However, the best film for most interior shots is the very sharp daylight Kodachrome 200, which produces a pleasing color rendition from the usual mix of window and tungsten light. Combining wide-angle high-speed 24mm lenses with shutter speeds of 1/60 or 1/125 sec. and Kodachrome 200 will give you bright, crisp images.

Instinctively, many people think electronic flash will solve every indoor lighting problem they encounter. Although flash works in some situations, it rarely does an adequate job in large interiors. We've all seen lots of pictures taken with flash of people in large rooms where the background is totally black. The exposure may have been correct for the people in foreground, but the shutter speed commonly used with flash so underexposes the rest of the room that it turns black. Flash will often work when shooting a scene fairly close to a light colored wall, but it is important to make sure your flash has sufficient light output and will cover up to a 28mm lens. It is possible to shoot a combined exposure by flash and existing light with a slow shutter speed, but if your foreground subject is a person, he or she must remain as still as possible to avoid making a ghost image on the film.

Art

People have been motivated to create images since the dawn of time, and the world offers a broad spectrum of art. These products of the creative eye and mind can be seen everywhere in frescos, mosaics, paintings, sculpture, stained glass, and architecture. The task of documenting and interpreting great works of art is a challenge for the traveling photographer. Because our visual memories are such imperfect faculties, it is natural for us to want to preserve a vision of beauty. Of course, the photographic image is only a substitute for the original work of art, but it serves as a pleasant reminder of the initial experience. The smile of the Mona Lisa can affect us as much in a photograph as in the original painting.

Traveling photographers who record works of art in museums and art galleries are faced with technical problems such as lighting and exposure in addition to museum regulations that often ban electronic flash or tripods. In some cases, photography is prohibited al-

Art students spend days and even weeks copying a single painting in the Louvre. We wrote and took pictures for a story about copyists for Diversion *magazine.*

*This remarkable painting from the
tomb of an artisan exemplifies a break
from traditional religious art in Egypt.
The colors are still fresh and vibrant
after thousands of years. We took this
picture with electronic flash since the
only other illumination was from
handheld flashlights.*

together. Still, most major museums and galleries allow some form of photography in their hallowed halls. Technical advances in 35mm cameras, lenses, and film make it possible to take remarkably good pictures of paintings, sculpture, and artifacts. In fact, photographing art, and the gallery patrons who appreciate it, doesn't require expensive, specialized equipment but can be accomplished with the basic 35mm single-lens reflex or even a less expensive rangefinder or autofocus camera.

Having enough light is crucial for good art photography. Ideally, you should be able to work with soft daylight coming from windows or skylights. These conditions often exist in museums since this is also the best type of light for viewing art. Be aware, however, that daylight in museums is sometimes mixed with tungsten and/or fluorescent light. In most cases daylight color-transparency film is the best choice, but if artificial light predominates, you may need to use corrective filters to achieve an acceptable color balance in your pictures.

When the light level is relatively high with daylight as the predominant source, Fujichrome 50 or Koda-

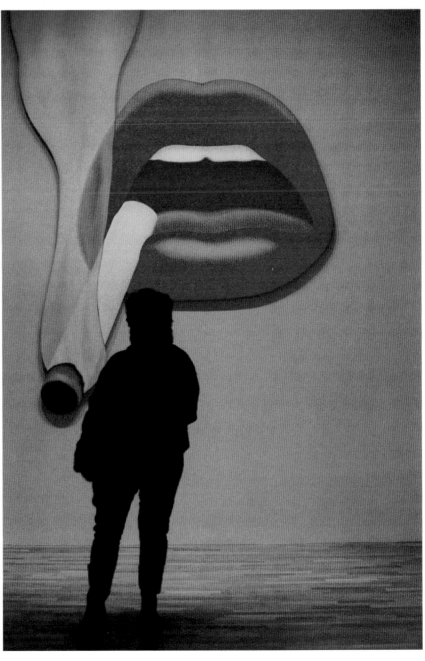

This is one of our favorite art museum pictures, taken at the Museum of Modern Art in New York City. The graphic simplicity of the image makes it a strong photograph.

chrome 64 is a good choice of film with a fast lens on your camera and a slow shutter speed. Most people hesitate to handhold a camera with shutter speeds slower than 1/30 sec., but 1/15 or even 1/8 sec. can be employed if you hold your breath and apply a steady hand. Often the camera can be braced against a wall or door jamb. The shutter-release button should be activated by a slow, steady pressure. If you punch the shutter button, your picture is likely to be blurred. If the light level is too low for Kodachrome 64 or Fujichrome 50, try Kodachrome 200. Under marginal light conditions it may be necessary to use Ektachrome 400, but this film will show discernible grain. The most successful lens for photographing art is the 35mm, a moderate wide-angle with a wide aperture. The standard 50mm lens is also a good choice, and it usually gives you the advantage of a wide aperture. These lenses are relatively free of linear distortion if held level with a painting.

When concentrating on the work of art itself, you must make some basic decisions. If your purpose is to accurately document the painting, you should include at least part of the canvas' frame to avoid eliminating any portion of its image. If your purpose is merely to create an interesting image from the painting, including the whole canvas is certainly not necessary; instead, you can show a broad area or focus in on a detail. Try showing both the art and the environment or gallery where it is displayed. People's reactions to art are interesting: a curious tilt of the head, an appreciative smile, or even a shocked expression in response to a mildly erotic bronze by Rodin.

It is frustrating to a photographer when a museum doesn't allow photography or imposes unreasonable restrictions. However, no one with consideration or sensitivity would want to obstruct the pleasure of others in art museums, so their limited restrictions in regard to photography are understandable. Most progressive museums, recognizing that art is meant to be shared, permit picture-taking without flash

or tripods. The Louvre in Paris, the Metropolitan Museum in New York, and the National Gallery in Washington, D.C. are just a few of the major museums that have this enlightened attitude.

Marketplaces

As you travel from country to country, you'll find that one of the most colorful and exciting places to take pictures is the local marketplace. Markets vary greatly in terms of what they sell, but they all have a common vitality. Open markets can be found anywhere in the world. Cities famous for them include Seattle, Hong Kong, Istanbul, Bombay, Bangkok, Rio de Janeiro, Athens, and Cairo. Most people think of markets in terms of food and produce, but many markets sell carpets, antiques, and brass and pottery wares in addition to, or instead of, edible commodities. Fortunately, for photographers, markets attract people; which makes the mix of subject matter richer and even more productive for picture taking.

The challenge, when photographing markets, lies in selecting and isolating the best images. Market backgrounds are often too busy. Even displays of food and merchandise can be a mass of different shapes and colors. There are several ways to solve this problem. One is to use a 70–210mm zoom lens with a wide aperture to throw the background out of focus. This selective-focus technique concentrates the viewer's attention on the point of interest you've chosen to be sharp.

Using a wide-angle lens offers a different solution, as it divides the picture into two separate planes. The foreground might be a pile of bright oranges or yellow bananas, while in the background, a woman behind the stand weighs fruit on a scale. Another useful technique is to focus very close on an interesting object on display such as a doll or a piece of dangling jewelry. Close up details are usually not strong travel pictures by themselves, but they can be very effective in a slide show that includes overall views of a market.

Look for graphic design and color in the marketplace, such as a swath

Marketplaces offer a wealth of photo opportunities to the traveling photographer. These bins of fruits and vegetables created neat patterns at the city market in Nairobi, Kenya.

This man sells his skills as a calligrapher in the street markets of Guangzhou in China. He uses both paints and ink to create colorful, artistic scrolls.

Our cameras captured the shy smile of a young woman (top left) in a street market in Xi Shuang Banna, China. By using a wide aperture on our lens, we were able to throw the background out of focus.

We recorded these glistening fish (bottom left) in the farmer's market in Seattle, Washington.

of brightly colored fabric or graphic characters on a poster or sign. Chinese calligraphy or Arabic script will make a picture seem even more exotic. Combine graphic elements to create your compositions of marketplaces, much as an abstract artist applies oil paint to a canvas. For example, try throwing background lights out of focus to create a dreamlike quality in your pictures.

Food

Don't forget to spoil yourself a little on every city shoot. Get plenty of rest and be sure to try some of the local culinary delicacies. After a day of walking in Rome, let your thoughts turn to a chilled bottle of Frascati wine and a dinner of mussels sauteed in garlic and tomato sauce over a bowl of pasta. Don't feel guilty; your strenuous exercise shooting great pictures has earned you the reward of a few Neapolitan calories, and sometimes the meal itself is a good subject for a picture.

Once in New Orleans, we decided to try eating Louisiana crawfish at a local restaurant. Those delicious little rascals, similar to miniature lobsters, are traditionally boiled in a peppery mix of herbs and spices. When our orders arrived, we simply had to photograph the bright red shellfish. Not only did the heaping platters look wonderful on Kodachrome, but we also enjoyed a sit-down, finger-lickin' feast after the shoot.

We can all take appetizing food pictures as we travel and dine. Shooting your own lunches or dinners may amuse waiters, cooks, and restaurant owners, but they rarely object, as the cooking and serving of fine food is an art, much like photography. People take pride in what they do well, and they are pleased to have their efforts recognized.

If the food is illuminated by natural daylight, try using Fujichrome 50 or Kodachrome 64. Unless you're dining alfresco, it is wise, during daylight hours, to select a table near a window. Very low light levels present a problem, but there are ways to cope with it. The best solution is to use a table-top tripod with a cable release on the camera.

Less conspicuous than full-size tripods, table-top models won't trip your waiter or give heart palpitations to the maitre d'.

The choice of a lens for food pictures depends on your purpose and selected subject. A wide-angle lens can provide you with a focal point of interest in the foreground while maintaining sharp focus in the background. This might be, for example, a careful foreground arrangement of pâté de foie gras, caviar, and chilled artichokes next to an ice bucket of French champagne, with a window view of the Cathedral of Notre Dame and the Seine River in the background. Using a normal 50mm or moderate 80–150mm telephoto lens will give you the option of selective focusing at a wide aperture. Your sharply focused subject should be something with defined linear qualities, such as a glass of wine or a piece of fruit.

There is definitely a correlation between visual stimulation and appetite. Sunlight sparkling through a tall-stemmed goblet of wine makes a beautiful and enticing visual image. The spectral highlights in the glass can be enhanced with a star-burst filter that turns each highlight into a tiny star. Japanese specialties are often masterpieces of art and design. For example, sushi is made from rice and raw fish, each piece crafted with care and arranged on a dark lacquer tray. The finished product is best photographed directly from above to show the careful and artistic arrangement of the various visual elements.

From time to time, especially when dining after dark, electronic flash may be necessary. Bring along a coil extension cord for using the flash off-camera, usually handheld above the camera to the left and directed at the subject. One light source is an obvious limitation and a second strobe can be converted to a slave, by the addition of an inexpensive electric eye on the hot shoe attachment of the second unit. The light from the camera flash automatically triggers the slave. This slave can be held by your dinner companion, to provide a side or back light in addition to the camera strobe.

Taking flash pictures in a restaurant can be disconcerting, so it is always courteous to ask the maitre d' for permission.

On your next trip around the corner or around the world, turn your attention and your camera to the subject of food. You'll probably find some compelling images, perhaps a golden-brown loaf of French bread, a plate of fruit in your hotel room, or a steaming bowl of bouillabaisse at a sidewalk café along the Riviera. What you eat on vacation can also be food for thought as well as photography.

Food is an important aspect of travel that we both enjoy and photograph with pleasure. This platter of Cajun country crayfish in Louisiana was especially delicious.

We used our camera to preserve the memory of a delightful lunch (shown at left) at the Golden Flower Hotel in Xian, China. The picture was taken with electronic flash, but we were able to preserve detail in the background by using a relatively slow shutter speed.

CHAPTER 4

Focusing on People

We photographed a woman in Tanzania balancing a bag of millet on her head and used her red African-print scarf to accent the foreground. The background is soft and out of focus, which concentrates attention on the subject.

Photographers are often afraid to photograph people, especially people they don't know. It isn't hard to see why; cameras to some degree do invade people's privacy. In foreign countries, photographers should be even more sensitive to people's feelings because they don't speak the language and can't explain why they want to take someone's picture. It is a mistake, however, to assume that all people will object to having their pictures taken. A delicate approach is the key. Professional travel photographers on assignment must come back with good people pictures in addition to shots of scenics, buildings, and monuments, because people are a vital part of any comprehensive location coverage.

Finding the Right Approach

Much depends on the approach you use in photographing people. A friendly smile always works to your advantage, and don't hesitate to use sign language in a foreign country. You'll be surprised by the number of people who'll agree to pose for the camera, but don't be discouraged if you get turned down now and then. Continue on your way; another subject is bound to be more cooperative. The very fact that you want to take someone's picture shows a personal interest that is flattering to most potential subjects.

There are two sure-fire methods for photographing strangers. The

first is to find an interesting-looking family with a young child or baby. Admire the youngster and indicate that you'd like to take his or her picture. Proud parents are almost always glad to let you photograph their children, and after the ice is broken, the entire family may be willing to pose for you.

The second approach is to carry an instant camera, such as the Polaroid Spectrum, in addition to your SLR. Shoot a Polaroid picture and give this to your subject as a present. Watching the photograph develop is especially interesting to people in foreign countries where instant cameras are not common. People are invariably fascinated by their own image, and in this case it will work to your advantage. Once you've given them a picture of themselves, most people are willing to pose for your regular cameras.

Under some circumstances you may want to take strictly candid pictures of people. One method is to use a telephoto zoom, such as a 70–210mm lens. With this lens in the telephoto position, you can stand back a considerable distance and make relatively closeup shots of people. Often they won't notice that their pictures are being taken. The point-and-shoot technique is another method. Put your camera and a wide-angle lens on a strap around your neck and hang the camera about chest level. At close range and with a prefocused lens aimed at the

The white design on this Tanzanian boy's face indicates that he had just recently been circumcised. Including such cultural details in captions piques viewer interest.

The key to photographing strangers is to admire their children, especially in China (top left). Proud parents rarely object to having their children photographed, even when you can't speak the language.

In marketplaces we often take pictures of people absorbed in their own activities. This East African woman (bottom left) was carrying a large stalk of green bananas. We used a wide aperture to throw the background out of focus.

intended subject, trip the shutter without raising the camera to your eye. This technique works very well in a crowded marketplace or street. The new autofocus cameras make chest-level shooting much easier and more accurate. Yet another technique involves a mirror attachment for the lens that allows you to point your camera in one direction while actually taking the picture in another. (The mirror device, called the Circo Mirrotach, is available from Spiratone Photo Supplies, 135-06 Northern Boulevard, Flushing, New York 11354.)

Although it is generally preferable to photograph people candidly, they are often willing to pose. We once found a man dressed as a town crier on Portobello Road in London, and he was delighted to pose for us. We've been able to convince people to pose in the free markets of China by using sign language. We often try to explain to subjects why we want pictures of them, and tell them, for instance, that we like the bright color of their clothing, or that the effect of the sun on their hair. When people understand your purpose, they rarely object to being photographed; instead, they often become excited and involved in the creative process with you.

In some countries photographing people is very difficult, and you may even encounter hostility from potential subjects. This is especially true in the Middle East and Africa. There, the solution is to shoot candidly and hope your subject is unaware of the camera. Even if we take someone's picture without his or her knowledge, we feel strongly that pictures of people should never hold anyone up to ridicule. At the same time, remember that in fact many people enjoy having their picture taken. Your purpose is to document an interesting aspect of life. Don't let what may be natural shyness make you miss great people pictures.

When we are traveling, we consider it a special treat to be invited into someone's home. If we are asked to do a portrait, we like to put the subject against a wall or backdrop and use special lighting equip-

ment (see "Electronic Flash Units" in chapter 1). However, flood lights and electronic flash are distracting for your subjects, and artificial light often destroys the natural quality of the photograph. Personally, we prefer to shoot candid portraits in natural daylight, even if what we want to achieve is a flattering or romantic picture. Available or existing light is the best possible illumination for photographing people, so try to do your portrait work outside or near a window. Kodachrome 64 is a good daylight film for portraiture, and Kodachrome 200 is an ideal film for less-than-perfect light situations.

Certain techniques are good for creating special-effect illusions in portraiture. Seamless paper backdrops curve where they meet the floor and can be used to make the subject appear to float in space. If you can't buy seamless paper easily nearby, go to a marketplace and purchase two yards of plain, wide material. It is important that this cloth should be able to absorb light and not bounce it. Wool, therefore, is much better than taffeta. Putting Vaseline around the edges of a clear filter will soften and blur the edges of your picture. Diffusion filters will do the same thing more evenly to the entire picture. Colored filters are good for warming up skin tone, and starburst filters can be used to create a small bright diamond in each eye (see "Filters" in chapter 1).

A basic fault with many amateur pictures is that they aren't taken close enough to the subject. Don't be afraid to move in close. Most adjustable cameras can focus down to 3 or 3½ feet, and the best people pictures are usually made at this close range. A 70–210mm zoom lens is helpful for capturing an intimate moment between two people without intruding too much into their private space.

Focal lengths in the range of 70–150mm bring a flattering perspective to human subjects. The best focal length for portraits is approximately 90mm. Wide-angle lenses tend to distort faces in the near foreground. Whatever lens you use, have your subjects lift their chins

This portrait of an Alaskan Chilkat Indian wearing a ceremonial headdress and a nose ring makes a strong statement about an ancient culture. The picture was made on a dark, overcast day, so it was necessary to photograph the subject against the sky for contrast.

Closer is better when you are taking stock shots of people. This man (shown at left) in Kunming, China, was amused that we wanted to photograph him.

It is often effective to frame your subject against the clear, uncluttered background of the sky. In this case we photographed an Indian guide in Venezuela from a low angle and from behind, stressing the strong graphic quality of the picture instead of a face.

just a fraction of an inch. This will take five pounds and five years off their appearance. Also have them look at something just beyond you and slightly taller than you are. This will put a sparkle of light and liveliness into their eyes.

Spend some time talking with the subjects you are going to photograph. Watch the light play on their hair and skin and move them around until you find the best angle. As you converse, you'll see their expressions change. Try to channel the conversation to fix the mood expression you want. We like to take advantage of any natural prop we find. For example, if a subject smokes a pipe, we photograph him against a dark wall so that the pipe's curling smoke becomes part of the design in the picture.

If a suitable background isn't apparent, get down low and photograph your subjects against the sky, but do be careful that the camera doesn't take its exposure reading off the sky. If you don't have a spotmeter, then compensate for a bright sky by setting your exposure dial at +1. Conversely, if your background is extremely dark or shadowed, try bracketing your exposures with a −1. If lack of natural light means that a flash unit must be used, hold the flash head away from your camera. This way you won't get "red-eye" portraits of your subjects or dark shadows behind them. If the background is a white or off-white wall, you can aim your flash head so that its light bounces off the wall and indirectly onto your subject, which adds a soft, flattering effect. You can use the same bounce technique against a white ceiling or nearby side wall.

The most desirable times of day to shoot outdoor portraits are in the early morning and the late afternoon when the sunlight is warm and at a low angle. Avoid high noon if possible since direct, overhead light causes harsh, unflattering shadows. If you must shoot in the middle of the day, use reflected light, such as flash fill, to soften the shadows. A reflector can be made from a large piece of white cloth, held at a low angle so that sunlight is reflected on

Electronic flash can be used in daylight to fill in deep shadows on a person's face. This technique is called "synchro-sun." Some cameras and flash units are designed to compute and balance daylight and flash output automatically. If your flash unit offers you a choice of power settings, choose a lower setting for closeup portraits. We photographed this woman and her bright earrings at the Sunday market in Xi Shuang Banna, China.

Bright sunlight presents special problems when taking pictures of dark-skinned people, especially during the middle of the day. This portrait of a herdsman in Upper Volta was made by filling in the details of his face with electronic flash. We were careful not to let the flash overpower the existing sunlight.

to the face. Aluminum foil can also be used, but the reflected light will not be as soft or natural as the light reflected from a white cloth.

Portraits should reflect your subjects' personalities, but it's also interesting to see their interaction with the environment. This might be teenagers frolicking in the surf at the beach, Aunt Ellen studying a Rodin statue, or a child learning to ride a bicycle. Whatever the circumstances, strive to keep your subjects looking animated and occupied. There is nothing more boring than a lifeless portrait against a lifeless monument. Always try to feature the unique qualities of your subjects. Choose people with interesting faces or shoot people in such a way as to make their portrait meaningful to viewers. If you've been shy about photographing people, decide to be an extrovert with your camera and become a connoisseur of the faces of the world. Once you've tried photographing people, you'll be surprised how easy it is, and you may even make some new friends along the way.

Portraying Children

Pictures of people interacting with their environments are particularly appealing when they include children or animals. Youngsters have a way of expressing their feelings without inhibition. Children aren't restricted by the barriers that sometimes exist between adults, which may explain the universal appeal of child photography. They are the most widely photographed subjects in the world. Thousands of miles of film are exposed each year by proud parents who record their offspring kicking off their blankets, crawling out of their cribs, falling off their tricycles, and toddling off to kindergarten. Traveling photographers should always be ready to anticipate moments when children are just being themselves.

Young children don't understand the concept of posing, so your best pictures of them will be candid shots in which the child is absorbed in activity or play. This doesn't mean you can't guide and direct your subject in a subtle way. You can

Because the scene of the Chinese mother feeding her baby with chopsticks was strongly backlit, we increased our exposure by one stop to provide detail in their faces. The white bowl served as a natural reflector to brighten the child's features.

These young boys in Mombasa, Kenya, responded with unbridled enthusiasm to having their picture taken. Don't be put off if children mug for the camera. Take the picture anyway; you may come up with a winner.

A photographer must always be ready to catch the spontaneous reaction of children. During an assignment in China, we photographed three little boys (shown at right) and captured a wonderful expression.

often suggest an activity or game, and then let the youngster proceed on her own while you keep your camera ready for action as the picture situation develops. This sometimes leads to a series of excellent pictures that are entirely different from what you had originally planned.

Another unexpected reward of watching children as you travel is the opportunity to record children's spontaneous reactions to the adult world. If you are at a crowded scene of some loud or rough activity (for example, sheep dipping in Australia), your best photograph may be the one shot behind a small child including the child's reaction in the foreground of your picture.

A sensitive photographer can often see a potentially good picture getting ready to happen. For instance, a child's reaction to a new pet might develop into a good subject. The relationship between family members of different generations is usually a rewarding subject for the camera. Again, keep the picture situation as free and natural as possible.

Another approach is to determine the picture you would like to capture and then situate yourself in the spot where it is most likely to happen. Playgrounds and parks often yield pictures of children oblivious to their environment. Outdoor markets and fairs are also

promising locales for such pictures. For example, you could select a display of bright shrimp or flower stalls for the foreground and then compose a colorful photograph showing vendors, customers, parents, and children. For this type of shot you need a wide-angle lens, perhaps a 24mm, for focusing on your foreground and keeping the background sufficiently sharp.

Working with Models

Most amateur or traveling photographers don't think about using models, but anyone who poses for a camera is a model and a glamorous scenic often benefits from adding a human element. This could be a member of your own family, or a willing stranger. Here are a few helpful guidelines for choosing models:

• Select attractive, interesting people who have an easy manner and won't be self-conscious in front of a camera. Although young people and even children make good models, don't confine yourself to youth.

• Whenever possible, have your models wear vivid, lively colors.

• Photographing your traveling companion is an ideal way to add warmth and interest to your scenic pictures.

• Posing two people together usually makes a more interesting pic-

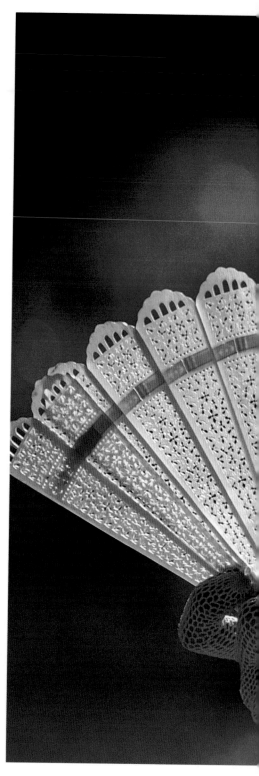

Here we posed an attractive waitress near Chinese lanterns in a restaurant in Xian, China. The red tassels provided a spot of color.

Backlighting your subject is an interesting way to do a portrait. We positioned this model in the late afternoon sun so that it illuminated her fan. Our exposure still retained the shaded detail in her face.

GETTING MODEL RELEASES

Model releases for pictures of people are usually not needed for editorial use in textbooks, magazines, and newspapers. Neither are property releases for pictures of houses or other property. If, however, an advertising agency wants to use a photograph in an ad, having a model or property release is obligatory. Therefore, it always makes sense to try to get one when you shoot.

Model-released slides should be marked with a small red "R" in the upper right-hand corner of the slide mount. Model and property releases should be carefully filed according to location and date so that they are easily accessible. Be wary of keeping any photograph that ridicules or demeans the subject. If it is published and there is a legal action, you'll end up in court, whether you arranged for a model release or not.

Every photographer seems to use different language in his or her model release. The *ASMP Professional Business Practices in Photography* guidebook, published by the American Society of Magazine Photographers, has some good suggestions for wording model releases. Ours is printed on 3 × 5-inch cards to fit in our camera bags and reads:

"I hereby give photographers Carl and Ann Purcell, their legal representatives and assigns, the right and permission to publish, without charge, photographs of me, _____ taken at _____. These pictures may be used in publications, audio-visual presentations, promotional literature, advertising, calendars or in any other manner. I hereby warrant that I (or undersigned Parent/ Guardian) am over eighteen (18) years of age, and am competent to contract in my own name in so far as the above is concerned."

Below this are spaces for the date, the model's or parent/ guardian's signature, address, telephone number, and the dated signature of a witness.

When we are getting model releases from strangers, we always give our subjects one of our business cards so that they know who we are. We usually promise to send prints to them at the addresses they give us on the model releases. When we get back home and process the film, we are always careful to follow up and send the prints we promised.

Whether you use models or strangers, it is important to acknowledge that your people pictures may well be the most meaningful images you'll ever take as a photographer. A view of people, their emotions, and their interaction with their environment will evoke far more sentiment in your audience than most scenics. Your reactions to people and your feelings about them will also be exposed.

Certain people pictures have special meaning for us. This young couple at the Temple of the Jade Buddha in Shanghai is lighting candles and praying for the birth of a male child. China strongly advocates only one child per couple, and most families hope and pray for a male heir.

We recorded the classic profile of the young Kikuyu woman in Kenya (shown at left) by exposing for the background and letting her face become a silhouette.

ture than a single person. Personal interaction is the key to better people pictures. Encourage your models to do something together and to laugh and talk. Try to help them forget the camera. Mix and match generations: for example, photograph two older people enjoying a rose bush, or pose a grandmother showing a flower to her grandchild.

Don't hesitate to ask nonprofessionals to pose for your camera. Most people will be pleased and flattered that you consider them attractive enough to be models. It takes some special skills to bring out the best in amateur models. They often feel awkward and don't know how to stand, and they will rely on your easy-going authority to direct them into effective compositions. The first thing to do is to place your model in good light. Ideally, the model will be facing the light source, but facing direct sunlight may force models to squint, and this is not a flattering expression. In such cases, move your models to open shade or at least position them so that they don't look directly into the sun. An alternative is to put the sun behind your models and rimlight their hair, but with this kind of backlighting it is necessary to take a closeup exposure reading directly off the face. Chat with your models and encourage them to think happy thoughts. The goal is to make all the elements of the composition come together so that you take the picture in that fleeting moment.

Working with models can greatly improve your travel pictures. You should use them carefully, positioning them in the most appropriate place in your composition to make an effective visual statement. Models don't have to be prominent elements in your pictures, but they will always add human interest and scale.

CHAPTER 5

Photo Opportunities

People in the Third World work long, hard hours just to grow enough food to live. This field worker in China is shown planting rice seedlings in the cool light of an early morning.

The world is our studio, and we explore it with an avid interest. The travel environment, however, rarely offers us the complete control available in a studio, but we consider this lack of control an advantage in creating spontaneous images as they flow through time and space. If it rains, we capture drops of water on a girl's face or a sea of bright umbrellas in a marketplace. If the light is not right, we wait until it is. Each season of the year offers different problems and different visual opportunities. We use our talent and skill to take advantage of these opportunities and create images of lasting value.

Dawn

Dawn is a very special time for a photographer. It heralds a new day and provides a fresh and lovely light for pictures. We take pleasure in the hush of a spring morning when only the voices of birds can be heard. We have shared early morning in the Vale of Kashmir in northern India, on the Masai Mara plains of Kenya, and at a jungle shrouded temple on the island of Bali.

Just as memorable have been the mornings we have enjoyed sitting on the deck behind our house in northern Virginia. The deck overlooks nine miles of wooded parkland that falls off sharply to a winding brook. We warm our hands with steaming cups of coffee and watch the world come alive, our

cameras untouched for the moment. The morning sun will glisten on the dew-drenched, geometrical pattern of a spider web. Between the bright-green oak leaves we can see sparkles on the surface of the stream at the bottom of our hill. Cleo and Midnight, our dog and cat, romp together on the deep-piled carpet of the lawn.

Photographers should take the time to look at the world and study the play of light as it illuminates the environment in the first hours after sunrise. If the spirit moves you, then pick up your camera and record the image. Otherwise, file the image in your mind. It will usually be there for you to record the next morning or the morning after.

Morning light has a different quality from dusk and sunset when a deep orange from the aerial haze and dust hangs near the horizon. Mornings tend to be clear. The sun is a pale gold, burnishing landscapes and foliage with the carefully crafted gold leaf of nature. At such a time you capture the magic of sunlight in a child's blonde hair or pinpoints of light in a dewdrop on a rose petal. From a technical standpoint, we often use a macro lens for closeups and like to backlight our subjects with the morning sun. Fujichrome 50 has the ability to enhance the greens of leaves and grass.

Spotmetering with either your camera or a handheld meter will enable you to achieve color detail in

New York City's Central Park at dawn in winter is a frozen fairyland. We took this picture from the seventeenth floor of the Ritz Carlton Hotel on Central Park South to capture the city's skyline tipped by the morning sun.

It is easy to understand why Monument Valley in Arizona is a sacred place to the Navajo Indians. We rose before the first light to reach a vantage point at the Visitor's Center overlooking the valley. As we were taking our pictures, we saw this lonely minibus driving toward us, the massive shape of El Capitan in the distance.

the area of your choice. If you don't have a spotmeter, move in close for your reading and lock the exposure (see your camera manual) and move back to recompose. We would point out, however, that some photographers using spotmetering tend to overexpose and wash out highlight detail. Center-weighted metering will cover most scenes, even those with back light.

For several years we have traveled to Monument Valley in Arizona during the month of October. This area, sacred to the Navajos, with its magnificent buttes and mesas is a very special place at dawn. We always pull ourselves out of bed at Goulding's Lodge while it is still dark and drive to the visitor's center which overlooks the valley, setting up our tripods on the ridge. The sky turns from black to a deep purple, and gradually the horizon becomes a lip of rose. The mesas are Rorschach

ink blots against the morning sky. One never knows when the perfect moment will arrive, but our cable releases are ready and every few minutes we expose a frame and our motor drives advance the film. Ironically, a sunrise can often be enhanced by using a Cokin graduated sunset filter. If the sun has risen too high and the scene is too hot, it can be toned down with this filter, but the picture will still retain details in the foreground. Another useful filter for sunrise is amber colored.

On your next journey we hope you will get up early enough to discover the beauty of dawn. It could be on an island in the Caribbean, in a mountain meadow of blooming wild flowers in the Swiss Alps, or amid the terraced rice fields of southern China. The world is a wonderful and exciting place in the morning, and you'll miss some great pictures if you stay in bed.

Sunsets

Some photographers chase rainbows. We're forever chasing sunsets. There is a special, almost magical quality to sunlight late in the day when that giant orb starts to sink below the horizon. The setting sun symbolizes tranquility, a feeling of peace at the day's end in a world too often filled with deadlines and schedules.

Photographing sunsets is not always as simple as it appears. Most autoexposure cameras can't cope with the direct sun in the picture frame. Shooting directly into the sun causes their built-in exposure meters to underexpose most of the scene. Because most autoexposure cameras have center-weighted metering systems, positioning the sun away from the center of the frame is a good idea. In addition, pictures of sunsets often benefit from setting your exposure-compensation dial at +1. A semiautomatic or match-needle camera can be adjusted by simply opening the aperture one additional stop.

Proper exposure can also be obtained by taking a direct reading from the sky after the sun has dipped below the horizon. At that point the sun won't confuse the exposure meter since the light in the sky and surrounding clouds is relatively even. It is always wise with any sunset picture to bracket your exposures so that you'll get the best color saturation possible. Also, tripods or beanbags are often necessary to steady telephoto lenses for sunset exposures.

A sunset is more dramatic and more interesting when there is something or someone in the foreground as a point of interest. If you want, electronic flash can be used to illuminate the people in the foreground. You'll need to balance the background light of the sunset with

We love to shoot sunsets, and our best shots include a point of interest in the foreground. We waited on Mallory Square Pier in Key West until this schooner sailed across the sunset; then we shot the scene with a 400mm lens. The sun seems impaled like a golden apple on the prow of the ship.

At the peak of an ancient volcano on the island of Bartolome in the Galapagos, Ann posed for this picture. The sunset was enhanced with a Cokin graduated sunset filter.

the light from your flash. This requires careful planning. You should arrange your models and put your camera with a cable release attached on a tripod at least fifteen minutes prior to exposure. Use a slow-speed film such as Kodachrome 64, and wait until the sun is well below the horizon and the natural light level is low. Then do a time exposure of several seconds at an aperture of $f/8$ or $f/11$. This procedure will let you pick up colors in the evening sky that can barely be seen with the naked eye.

Fire your flash unit with the manual control during the few seconds that the shutter is open. Using auto-exposure flash is fine, but set the ISO on the flash unit a bit higher than normal to provide a more subtle amount of artificial light. Employing this professional trade secret can create some very dramatic sunset pictures when executed properly.

What can be done to enhance the colors of a sunset when nature needs a little help? Fortunately, filters are available for adding a spark of color to a bland sunset; however, simply slapping an orange filter over your lens usually produces pictures that look painfully artificial. Cokin produces a special graduated sunset filter that is more effective. The top of the filter is deep orange, and the filter fades to pale orange at the bottom. Using it will turn any sky into a dramatic sunset while preserving the natural color of details in the landscape's foreground. Auto-exposure SLR cameras compute their exposures directly through the lens and filter, making manual computation of the filter's exposure factor unnecessary.

You need the right lens to capture a sunset effectively. A telephoto in the range of 200–500mm will make the orb of the sun appear larger than it does to the eye. The most dramatic sunset pictures taken with telephotos juxtapose something, such as a boat, a sail surfer, or a pelican resting on a piling, with the setting sun. A wide-angle lens is more effective for showing the broad sweep of the sky after the sun sinks below the horizon. Any focal length from 18–35mm can be used,

We came across this couple sitting on a wall in the sunset on the island of Hydra in Greece. They agreed to pose, and just as we were about to take the picture, a friendly dog jumped up on the wall to get the woman's attention.

but the wider the lens, the more important it is to keep your camera level with the horizon to prevent linear curvature. Always check that the horizon line is level, just before you press the shutter button.

The best thing about sunsets is that they can be found anywhere. Wherever you may be at the end of the day, if you turn your camera to the west, you may capture a priceless moment in time and space, whether you are in the Greek islands or in your own backyard.

Night

After the sun goes down, many photographers put away their cameras. Most cities at night, however, are alive with light; many buildings, fountains, and monuments are illuminated. Dramatic travel pictures can be taken of urban night scenes by following a few basic guidelines.

Oddly enough, daylight color film produces the best night pictures because city lights comprise a mixture of neon, tungsten, and quartz. Daylight color film renders this mixture in warmer, more pleasing tones than tungsten film, which tends to be bluish and cold when recording outdoor scenes at night. Good hand-held exposures can be made at night with some of the new high-speed films, such as Kodachrome 200. We prefer however, to use slow-speed color-transparency films, such as Kodachrome 25 or 64 or Fujichrome 50, and a time exposure of ten to twenty seconds with the camera on a tripod. A high-speed film is not necessary when you make a time exposure using a good tripod and a cable release, plus a slower film's high resolution is preferable to a faster film's inherent graininess.

After gathering the right equipment and film, your next step is to select a subject in a brightly lit area. The mixed light sources will either be direct or reflected. Neon tubes and street lights are examples of direct-light sources; an illuminated building would be a reflected-light source for your film. Neither kind of illumination is superior to the other, so when selecting subjects, all you have to worry about is what is

visually pleasing and interesting.

In many instances your night subject will be an illuminated building or monument and a street with traffic in the foreground. Don't be apprehensive about recording moving lights during time exposures; the headlights and taillights of cars in motion create fascinating patterns in time-exposure pictures and add far more to a composition than they detract. Time exposures at night make moving lights look like tracer bullets or red-and-white lines so that streets become rivers of color, visual essays on movement and time.

Getting an accurate light reading in such a confused conglomerate of light and dark is less difficult than you might expect. If your autoexposure camera has an aperture-priority mode, set your aperture at f/5.6. This aperture provides the best resolution for most lenses and

lets the camera make an educated guess as to the right exposure, and in most instances its choice will be within the acceptable range for a good exposure. Just be sure that the camera is solidly mounted on the tripod and that you use the cable release without the locking device. Exposures in most nighttime city scenes run between five and fifteen seconds with Kodachrome 64. You'll hear the shutter close at the end of the exposure.

Bracket your exposures by shooting two extra frames even when using autoexposure. Give one frame one stop overexposure (+ 1) and the other one stop underexposure (− 1). Many cameras have a special exposure-compensation dial for bracketing. If yours does not, just reset your ISO for one stop difference both ways.

If your camera doesn't have aper-

The United States Capitol and its Christmas tree are shown reflected in the ice of a frozen pond. This picture was made with a camera on a tripod and a short time exposure on Fuji-chrome 50.

The best time to take night shots is just after sunset when there is still a trace of ambient light left in the sky. We made this picture of the Golden Gate Bridge in San Francisco using a tripod and a twenty-second time exposure. The taillights and headlights of the moving cars were recorded on Koda-chrome as red-and-white streaks.

A Finnish field of rapeseed flowers, accented by sunlight, contrasted with the ominous slate-gray sky of an approaching storm and created a graphic image suitable for a poster. It is often helpful to visualize our pictures in terms of design elements. Selective focusing of your subject and cropping in the viewfinder allows you considerable creative control over the final image.

ture priority or is an older model that lacks autoexposure settings, you'll have to use a cable release that has a locking device. Again, set the aperture at $f/5.6$, but set the shutter-speed dial on "B." Compose your picture with the camera on the tripod, open the shutter with the cable release, and lock it open for the duration of the time exposure. When using Kodachrome 64 to shoot a typical urban night scene, expose one frame for two seconds, another frame for four seconds, and a third frame for ten seconds. If the scene is darker than normal, you may want to expose a fourth frame for twenty seconds.

Take the time to try new approaches. For example, a person or object in the foreground of a night picture can be illuminated by manually firing an electronic flash during the time exposure. The flash should be just a bit underexposed to give light-colored clothes and flesh tones good color saturation. Elaborate and expensive camera equipment is not necessary to take good outdoor pictures at night. Much more important is your willingness to experiment with exposures and the ability to visualize the way they will appear on film.

Foul-Weather Photography

We instinctively associate photography with sunlight. Too many photographers pack away their cameras when the clouds block out the sun and run for cover at the first sprinkle of rain. This is a sad mistake; there are many beautiful and compelling images in the rain, fog, and snow. A bright but cloudy day can provide a soft, pleasing light without harsh shadows. Keep your camera out and you'll come up with some very worthwhile pictures.

One of the biggest problems of taking pictures in foul weather is getting acceptable color rendition when using color film. Many scenes appear drab and lifeless in gray light, but with a little creative planning you can add the needed color. A bright red firetruck or a yellow raincoat can make a dull picture sparkle with life. The very contrast between the vivid color and the gray

background is visually exciting. Sometimes you will find the needed color in nature, such as a vivid red rose in a rainy English garden.

In this world of color television and movies we often overlook the medium of black and white. In many ways black and white film is ideal for foul weather pictures. It is generally faster (more sensitive to light) than our old standby, Kodachrome. Since black-and-white film records only shades of gray, there is no problem with color loss; indeed, black and white enhances and takes advantage of the somber mood of an overcast or rainy day. Some photographers, especially those working in the documentary and art fields, prefer the purity of the black-and-white medium to color. Part of the creative control they exercise with black and white depends on custom developing and printing.

In spite of their ethereal beauty, clouds sometimes dump light sprinkles or heavy downpours on you. This may not inspire you to do Gene Kelly's "Dancing in the Rain" number, but there are still picture opportunities if you can protect your cameras and know what to look for. The most obvious way to protect your cameras is with an umbrella, but holding an umbrella and operating a camera at the same time is not easy. One ingenious photographer fitted an umbrella with a camera bracket that could be adjusted on the vertical shaft and tightened in place with a screw or clamp.

Another protective device is the Ewa-Marine, a clear plastic bag with a watertight seal. The bag has a built-in glove that allows the photographer to manipulate the controls for focusing, film advance, and shutter release. The glove models of the Ewa-Marine are quite expensive, but they can also be used underwater at depths up to one-hundred feet and are ideal for taking pictures on white-water rafting trips or on any boat where a camera might be exposed to water. (Ewa-Marine is distributed by Pioneer Marketing Research, Inc., in Westmont, New Jersey.) Ewa-Marine also makes a special plastic hood and rain cape

Don't get the rainy-day blues! Go out into the rain and look for bright, colorful subjects, such as these three girls in rain slickers. We used Fuji-chrome 50 to help accentuate the colors. The striped umbrella clearly says that it is raining even though you can't see rainfall in the picture.

Water in its many forms offers a multitude of photographic opportunities. This waterfall was shot in the jungles of Venezuela. Our shutter speed was fast enough to stop the action of the falling water.

designed with a small opening for a camera lens.

Another less expensive solution is to put the camera in a clear-plastic sandwich bag and close the opening around the barrel of the lens with a rubber band. (Be sure to use a clear glass or UV filter to protect the optical surface of the lens.) You can operate the controls through the flexible plastic and the camera stays dry, but the photographer gets wet.

What pictures might you find out there to take in bad weather? Perhaps you'll discover a horse and buggy, barely discernable in the London fog, or a sea of umbrellas on a rainy day in St. Peter's Square in Rome. A foul-weather picture could be as simple as a child sitting under a canvas tarp in the rain. Maybe you'll capture the excitement of a snow storm in Switzerland. We don't pretend that foul weather offers as many picture opportunities as sunshine, but it is surely a mistake to pack away your camera and not seek out the images that are available.

Water

So much of the world is covered by water that it is not surprising that this element is a common subject for photography. Water does wonderful things with light. It shines, reflects, sparkles, and shimmers in the rays of the sun. On a foggy day water vapor diffuses sunlight into soft, muted pastels. A single drop of morning dew on a cobweb can catch the golden light of dawn and reflect the world as a tiny jewel of nature. You can capture such wonders in closeup detail by using a macro lens with your camera on a tripod.

Think of the many places you can find water. You've probably walked along beaches and seen the ocean in many moods: calm, placid, stormy, and turbulent. There is the water in streams, rivers, lakes, and ponds. The essence of photographing water depends on waiting for the right illumination, and this requires great patience. You can spend hours waiting for the sun to interact with clouds and water, but usually the pictures are well worth the wait.

Many photographers think light

reflecting off water is a problem. These reflections can be minimized or eliminated with a rotating polarizing filter, but removing them may not be desirable since the interaction of light and water is visually interesting. Consider the sun setting over the ocean. Under ideal conditions the sun creates a path of golden light across the water. Eliminate that marvelous reflection and you have a "ho-hum" picture. Use the reflection as a background for a windsurfer, and you have a great action shot. Put a young couple in the foreground at the base of the light's path, and a romantic mood is created. The number of ways you can incorporate reflections in your photographs is only limited by your imagination.

Reflections, or mirror images of reality, are also good photo opportunities provided by water. Wandering through Yosemite Valley in California, we once discovered a spot in a quiet river bend where Half Dome Mountain is beautifully reflected, especially at sunset. We found another nearly perfect reflection in a pool of water at Monument Valley in Arizona. A huge mesa, surrounded by buttermilk skies, was reflected in the water. Sometimes it is interesting to break up a reflection by dropping a pebble into a quiet pool and then photographing the concentric circles that result.

Clouds are a totally different form of water, and their vaporous shapes are good subjects for the camera. Various types of clouds such as cirrus, stratus, and cumulus can be made to stand out clearly against a blue sky by using a polarizing filter to darken the sky. Be careful not to let the sky turn dark navy blue by rotating the filter too far.

Water can also be a simple, uncluttered backdrop for your subject. A pretty girl in a pink bathing suit against the turquoise blue of the Caribbean creates a compelling contrast of color. There is usually an abundance of sunlight on open water and at beaches. Having such a strong light source means you can use a low-speed, high-quality color film such as Kodachrome 25 or Fujichrome 50. Even on a bright day,

you can create dark silhouettes of people on the beach by exposing the water in the background and letting the people's shapes go black against the bright water.

Using a fast shutter speed and wide aperture will throw your background out of focus and turn bright sunlight sparkling on water into a pattern of soft white light. A Cokin sunset filter will further transform it into floating pools of gold. A wide lens aperture can also turn sparkles on water into soft, luminescent globes of light, depending on the plane of focus. A starburst filter will turn each sparkle into a bright star.

The beach environment presents some special photographic problems. You'll want to use a slow- or moderate-speed color film, such as Kodachrome 25, Fujichrome 50, Kodachrome 64, or Kodacolor 100. Avoid high-speed color films with ISO ratings over 200. Some cameras don't have shutter-speed/aperture combinations that can handle high-speed films in very bright sunlight. Also, bright sunlight on white sand can fool built-in exposure meters. A girl in a bikini may appear underexposed, no matter how skimpy her bikini, if a white beach behind her overwhelms the exposure meter. This problem can be corrected either by opening up your aperture one stop or by using electronic flash to fill in the shadows.

Sand can cause serious damage to your cameras and lenses. At the beach your equipment and film should be kept in a closed camera bag in the shade to protect them from the sun's heat. When loading film, take extreme care not to get any sand in the camera. Spilled soft drinks can also really foul up a camera's mechanism; the advertising slogan "Things go better with Coke" certainly doesn't apply to photography equipment. You may be tempted to carry your camera into shallow water to shoot pictures of swimmers. Attempt this only in calm water and with great care. In case any salt water or salt spray gets on your camera, wash its surface with a cloth dampened in fresh water or alcohol, and then dry it with a clean towel.

A polarizing filter enhances white clouds and darkens blue skies on a clear day. Take care not to let your skies turn the color of blue ink.

Asking local residents where to find the best vantage point for specific pictures is often helpful. We asked one of the local photographers at Yosemite National Park for the best view of Half Dome Mountain at sunset. He guided us to a spot behind one of the lodges with a view across a small river.

We study our environment and are constantly alert for good pictures. We saw this stretch of beach on St. Lucia in the West Indies but waited until a solitary figure entered the scene before shooting.

When shooting at the shore, always carry a cleaning kit containing a small plastic bottle of alcohol, a small bottle of lens cleaner, lens tissue, a clean soft cloth, and cotton swabs for your camera equipment. Check your cameras and lenses each night, and clean them with a cotton swab and alcohol if necessary. Be sure to check and clean the pressure plate inside the camera as saltwater mist leaves a film.

Sailing with your camera can be an exhilarating experience, and you can get excellent picture results if you follow certain guidelines. Protect your cameras by putting them in plastic kitchen bags when you're not actually taking pictures. The precautions necessary for protecting your cameras will be determined in part by the weather. Don't overlook the "splash factor," stormy seas that can douse you and your equipment with corrosive salt water.

Fortunately, some cameras are designed for photography in and around water. The Nikonos, an underwater camera with a 35mm lens, can also be used above the surface. Other waterproof cameras include the Nikon Action Touch and the Minolta Weathermatic. Waterproof plastic housings with exterior controls, such as the Ewa-Marine products mentioned earlier, are available for some camera systems. Be sure to check to what depth the waterproof housing can go before it starts to leak.

Sunlight on open water is often harsh and leads to extreme contrasts between the white of the sails, the dark blue of the water, and shadow areas. Exposing for a middletone will give you the best results. When you take an exposure reading directly off a white sail, try using a +1 exposure factor, or opening up one stop, to keep the sails pure white.

If you want a bird's-eye view of the sailboat and the surrounding water, you'll have to climb to the top of the mast. In some sailboats you can be hoisted up in a sling seat.

Motor drives and autowinders are ideal for shooting action pictures at fast shutter speeds. This windsurfer was caught at a peak moment.

For a travel photographer, shooting on location might mean going a hundred feet beneath the ocean's surface to portray the sharp teeth of a giant moray eel. This picture was made with a Nikonos underwater camera and electronic flash at a coral reef off the coast of Jamaica. Note the waterproof housing on our subject's camera.

We climbed to the top of the radar mast to get an unusual, full-frame fisheye shot of the Sovereign of the Seas, *the world's largest cruise ship. We wanted to emphasize the enormous size of this impressive vessel.*

This can be a bit scary if the mast is pitching back and forth, but is relatively safe in calm water. A very wide-angle lens will help give you the all-encompassing view you want. A fisheye lens will even show the horizon in all four directions.

The movement of the water is exaggerated at the top of the mast, so you have to hold on to it with one arm, which leaves you only one hand for taking photographs. If you point the camera straight down from your eye, a wide-angle lens will include your feet in the picture. To avoid this you'll need to hold the camera as far away from your body as the camera strap allows; then watch where the lens is pointed so that you include the boat. Under these conditions, having a motor drive to advance your film is a great asset.

Leaning out from the side of a sailboat gives you an opportunity to create graphic images. Try framing different combinations of clouds,

the white wake, the hull of the boat, the sails, and the masts. The next time you are on a cruise ship, watch its wake at sunset. The water folds over the sky's reflected colors like golden velvet. Carefully compose the picture with a zoom lens from the ship's stern, and you may come up with a prize-winning image.

Snow

Images of snow can be found year around at high altitudes all over the world. A few basic rules can make these winter scenes as visually exciting as any taken in the tropics. First, you need to be careful when photographing snow if you are using an autoexposure camera. Large expanses of snow in the background can cause people or other subjects in the foreground to be underexposed. Before you take a picture, use your camera's exposure lock to read only the area of major interest. Also, white snow tends to appear dirty gray when exposed normally,

Winter conjures up images of a ski vacation. At this lodge in Rosegg Valley, Switzerland, a forest of skis and ski poles was planted in the snow.

so overexpose it by about one stop, or +1 on your exposure-compensation dial, to make it look pure white.

Photographing people wearing bright colors, such as red, can add a touch of interest to pictures taken on a cold, gray day. Ask your family or photography models to wear brightly colored sweaters, scarves, and stocking caps. Sunny winter days can create dark facial shadows. These can be eliminated by using fill light from an electronic flash or a tin-foil reflector. To make your own reflector, paste or tape some kitchen tin foil to a large piece of flat cardboard.

The romantic glow of a ski-lodge fireplace lasts a long time, but when you bundle up to go outside with your camera, your body quickly cools off. Dress warmly for your own comfort. You need to function at least as well as your cameras. Thermal underwear is a good idea. Layered clothing is effective and lets you take off one layer at a time if the day becomes warmer. Try wearing one or two wool sweaters under a Domke photography jacket. Its deep pockets carry extra film and lenses and its hood fits over a stocking cap. Wear one that covers your ears. Don't choose a hat with a brim or visor as it will get in your way when you lift your camera strap over your head. Wear gloves which will allow digital dexterity. Wool socks and comfortable shoes worn under rubber galoshes or rain boots will keep your toes warm. Sunglasses and sunscreen will protect you from snow glare and sunburn.

Camera batteries don't function well when they become very cold. You can keep them warm by carrying your camera under your coat and utilizing your body heat. Remember, as you return indoors to the fireplace, that your cameras are also cold and taking them into warm temperatures may cause some condensation on their metal and glass surfaces. Let the cameras and lenses warm gradually.

There are nonathletic ways to get spectacular winter photographs. For example, Swiss Railways has introduced an all-day excursion on the Glacier Express that gives you one breathtaking panorama after another enroute between Zermatt and St. Moritz. An added advantage for photographers is that the windows of this relatively luxurious train can be opened for picture taking. Don't pack a box lunch; for a very low price you can have a truly gourmet dining experience on the Glacier Express. In many countries cable cars have windows that don't open, but the ride usually deposits you at a spectacular vantage point for winter photography. Bring along a 70–210mm zoom lens to pick out individual houses or people on the hillsides.

Winter shots can be very beautiful. Look for light reflecting on ice-covered surfaces, or put the sun behind icicles and frozen tree branches. Take night photographs in cities whose frozen surfaces have become mirror images of colorful neon signs and traffic lights. Even during heavy snowfalls, you can put your camera in a clear plastic bag covering everything but the lens and go out walking. City lights, people, and traffic are transformed by swirling snowstorms into exotic photography subjects. Wherever you may be, hand the snowshovel to someone else, and grab your camera bag!

Autumn Foliage

The beautiful season of autumn understandably lures photographers into the forest and hills. The crisp air and natural beauty of the countryside will inspire you to new heights in recording and interpreting the fall colors outdoors. During late September and early October, Jack Frost dips his brush into a rich palette and turns much of the foliage in the northern hemisphere into a vivid display of various hues. The yellow, orange, and red leaves together offer a technicolor display rarely equaled in Hollywood. Mother nature often surpasses the fantasy of make-believe.

Where do you go to find the best display of autumn leaves? In America the foliage in the northern states is the first to turn, perhaps because the interlude between the warm and cold seasons is so brief. New England, and especially Vermont, is

well known for its autumn colors. However, you can find these colors anywhere throughout the United States north of the Mason-Dixon line. When the peak color arrives, it may last for only two weeks, and even local tourist boards cannot always accurately predict it. Exactly when autumn peaks is hard to say, so always have your camera ready to go during the autumn months.

In some areas autumn leaves create patterns of color across the hills or mountain ranges. A 70–210mm zoom lens is useful for compressing landscapes and pulling these patterns together into effective compositions. Shooting in bright sunlight is good to accentuate a group of colorful trees, but the muted colors that come from an overcast day can also produce appealing results on color film. For example, you could record a dramatic scene of colorful trees juxtaposed against slate-gray storm clouds. Autumn colors are also often enhanced by late-afternoon sunlight as it filters through the leaves, and backlighting this foliage can be very effective. Don't forget to move in close for some dramatic shots of individual leaves. Many modern lenses for SLR cameras have macro-focusing capabilities and can be used at close range. Try framing an image of sunlight filtering through a leaf, showing its coloration and fine veins.

People can play an important role in autumn compositions. A family outing in the woods is a natural source of models, and photographing a child as he discovers the beauty of a colored leaf is always delightful. Another possibility is to record several children playing in a pile of leaves as sunlight streams down through the forest canopy or to find a couple walking hand in hand through an autumn wonderland or raking and burning leaves in their yard. Electronic-flash

Autumn is an ideal season for photographers, but it takes careful planning to be at the right location when the leaves turn to deep gold and orange. This shot was made at Great Basin National Park in Nevada.

units are good for providing fill light when photographing people outdoors. Backlighting often leaves a person's face in dark shadow; then electronic flash can be used to bring out facial details.

A spotmeter is a useful tool for photographing foliage at a distance. There is a great difference in the amount of light reflected from dark-green leaves as compared to bright-yellow foliage. Using a spotmeter will give you an accurate reading from the most important area in an autumn scene. Remember that a telephoto zoom lens allows a built-in exposure meter to read only the area framed by the viewfinder, so to some extent, it acts as a spotmeter even if your camera lacks one.

Autumn offers a wide variety of subjects for photography. On farms, autumn is the time of year when many crops are being brought in from the fields. Harvesting is a fascinating activity to photograph, and even the crops themselves make good subjects. Imagine a pile of pumpkins modeled by the late-afternoon sunlight. How about pictures of children carving jack-o'-lanterns for Halloween? Try taking a closeup shot of a dried ear of multicolored Indian corn, or catch a farmer walking to his barn on a frosty morning. Show people with animals on the farm, such as a boy with his dog, a girl riding her horse through a meadow, or someone leading the cows back to the barn at the end of day. Autumn's colors are sure to enhance any photograph.

Shooting from the Air

Hundreds of thousands of passengers are carried daily by major airlines throughout the world, but manned flight is also for recreation and sightseeing. Tourists ride in helicopters over the Statue of Liberty, the Grand Canyon, and the Golden Gate Bridge. Enthusiastic amateur flyers ride the summer winds in hot-air balloons, hang gliders, and ultra-light airplanes. Private pilots fly their personal aircraft for vacation and business trips. Naturally, many aerial adventurers want to use their cameras to record the world from a bird's-eye view.

Fortunately, aerial photography doesn't require elaborate equipment or special film. Excellent pictures can be taken from the air with a standard SLR camera, any film, and a normal lens. There are a few ways to get satisfactory aerial pictures. On scheduled airflights you should carry your camera and film with you in a shoulder bag when boarding the aircraft. The x-ray machines at the security checkpoints in North America are not strong enough to damage or fog film with one exposure, but you should still ask for your film to be hand inspected by security personnel, which can be done easily and quickly if you keep your film in a clear plastic bag and remove it from your camera bag for inspection at the checkpoint.

When traveling by airliner, select a window seat that is not directly over the wing and with a clear view of the ground. Remember that your best pictures will be taken at a relatively low altitude, often shortly after take-off or before landing. You'll seldom get good aerial pictures from 30,000 feet. Shoot only on clear days when there is little or no ground haze, and try to use a shutter speed of 1/250 sec. to eliminate blur and keep your pictures sharp. Look for large clear compositional elements, such as mountain ranges or a city's tall buildings. Below 10,000 feet it is possible to get impressive pictures showing irrigated fields, river deltas, and erosion. Look for pattern and color in your viewfinder.

Remember that you're shooting through windows in an airliner. Often this causes a problem with reflection. The best way to eliminate these reflections is by using a rubber lens shade. Press it lightly against the window. This cuts out extraneous light as well as distracting reflections. A polarizing filter can also be used to eliminate reflections. Don't try to shoot with autofocus cameras that employ a sonar focusing system (such as a Polaroid camera) because it will focus on the windowpane. When in doubt, switch to manual focusing and focus on infinity if you have that option on your camera.

In addition to a normal 50mm lens, a moderate wide angle, such as a 35mm, is also useful, especially at lower altitudes. Since you are in a fixed position in your seat, zoom lenses can be very helpful by allowing you to crop your picture in the viewfinder for the most effective composition. There are some government restrictions on aerial photography and at airports, especially outside North America. You'll probably be warned in advance, but caution is advisable whenever there is any doubt.

Most guidelines for taking pictures from an airliner apply to shooting from a smaller aircraft, helicopter, glider, or hot-air balloon. One of the major advantages of taking pictures on these unscheduled flights is that if there are windows, they can usually be opened for an unobstructed view. Sometimes there aren't any windows. An ultra wide-angle 16–24mm lens can be effectively used in a balloon. Shooting upward from the gondola into the colorful nylon envelope makes a dramatic angle. On tourist helicopter flights be sure to request a window seat with a clear view for picture taking. It is always worthwhile to talk briefly with the pilot before take off and explain your needs as a photographer. Pilots usually understand the importance of light and angle and will cooperate whenever possible.

Most photographers think of aerial photography only in terms of looking downward at the earth. In fact, spectacular images can be composed of water vapor in the atmosphere. Vast layers of cloud formations often stretch as far as the eye can see. Most commercial flights are above these layers. Frequently, cumulonimbus cloud columns rise upward from the cloud base, and your flight may pass by them. Such clouds almost appear to have substance; others can be as delicate as feathers against the blue vault of the sky. Clouds take on a special beauty at sunset, turning golden and dream-like at the end of day. Be sure to bring your camera with you on your next flight so that you can start capturing these memorable pictures.

The top picture of a glider was taken by remote control with a motor drive and a full-frame fisheye lens on a camera that was firmly attached to the tip of the wing.

Get involved in your subject. If you're taking pictures of the Hot-Air Balloon Fiesta in Albuquerque, New Mexico, book a ride in a balloon. That is what we did to get this colorful balloon-to-balloon shot.

The bottom aerial shot of Lake Powell shows patterns of erosion in a natural abstract design.

CHAPTER 6

Selling Your Photographs

This view of Sugar Loaf Mountain in Rio de Janeiro was sold for $1,000 to Pan American Airlines as a poster.

Photography can be an expensive pursuit, especially travel photography, so it pays to put your photographs to work. Ideally, the income you generate from selling the reproduction rights to your travel pictures will reimburse you for the cost of your camera equipment, film processing, and duping as well as your travel costs and some of your living expenses.

There are several ways to earn money with your travel pictures. One is to sell your ideas to clients for assignments you then shoot. Another way is to sell usage rights to photographs you've already taken as part of the growing market of stock images used by editors and art directors around the world. The most substantial way to profit from your pictures is to put together an essay of words and photographs and market it as a feature article for newspapers or magazines. You are far more likely to make a sale to an editor if you can offer a complete package for publication.

Photography happens to be the way we make our living, and it is important to us to be paid well for what we do. This depends on our ability to take pictures that strike responsive chords in the creative directors at major magazines and advertising agencies. Our goal is to make these people feel the same visual excitement we felt when looking through the camera's viewfinder. That this creates a fairly high level of income for us is an important by-product of our creative process.

Getting Assignments

To get assignments you have to be good, but you also have to be willing to make appointments and knock on doors. The first step is creating a carefully prepared portfolio, something many photographers spend a lot of time and money preparing. One type of presentation involves using a large loose-leaf ring binder with vinyl sheets and black paper inserts. You mount your tear sheets of published work and your color prints in layouts on the black paper, insert these into the vinyl sheets, and place the sheets inside the binder. In addition, it is helpful to have some original 35mm transparencies in plastic sheets or a Kodak Carousel tray. Before having an appointment with a photo editor or art director, ask how he or she likes to view slides. An alternative type of portfolio consists of tear sheets, and/or color prints, laminated in 11 × 14-inch sheets, put inside a presentation box.

Don't be discouraged by rejection. As a travel photographer, you'll learn it comes with the territory. Not every editor or art director will like your work, but if you have talent, it will eventually be recognized.

When the great day arrives and you've been given an assignment, the question of your fee will come

It is rarely possible to predict the unusual ways your pictures will be used. We took this standard shot of the mutilated face of the Sphinx in Egypt. It later sold for $1,450 as an advertisement for plastic surgery.

up. The matter is far more complicated than you might expect. For example, editorial shoots are never as lucrative as advertising assignments. Regardless, your contract should always include your fee plus expenses. What do expenses include? Your office overhead is one of the expenses you might forget, but it should be included in your day rate. How much do you charge for a day lost because of rain? What rights should you give your client for the price charged? Will the company be able to use everything you shoot for any purpose, or should you give them a one-time use of any frame or multiple use of a specified number of pictures they've chosen? If you were shooting for a brochure and one of the pictures is later used on a billboard, did your contract have a clause about renegotiating other uses?

Your most reliable sources for answering such questions and negotiating the wording of an assignment contract is the *ASMP Guide to Business Practices*, a book published by the American Society of Magazine Photographers (ASMP). Headquartered in New York City, the ASMP has branches in major American cities. They also publish the *ASMP Stock Photography Handbook*, an indispensable guide on the subject of pricing assignments as well as stock photography. When determining your profits from an assignment, remember that the time spent shooting a job is usually only one-third the time actually involved. There is also time spent selling your artistic talent to the client in order to get the job; consulting with the client while negotiating your contract; planning the job; preparing the equipment; traveling to the job site and back; processing the film, and printing the results or dealing with the custom lab; meeting with the client to deliver the job; and finally, your time spent in bookkeeping and editing your slides.

In rare cases, some photographers do "work for hire," which results in the client owning the pictures outright. We strongly advise against such an arrangement, especially when shooting travel pic-

This peaceful sunset scene of Caneel Bay in the United States' Virgin Islands sold for $4,800 as a national institutional ad for a land development company.

One of our biggest stock sales resulted from a slide we almost threw away because it lacked color. These blowing palm trees in Tahiti, taken during a typhoon, sold to Nissan for an international ad for over $9,000. They wanted to illustrate the fact that their engineers studied wind to design cars.

tures, since the original images will have residual value in your personal stock file or at your picture agency. Some clients who are inexperienced in working with photographers will insist on retaining all rights to the pictures. Take the position that multiple or even unlimited use of the pictures can be negotiated, but that ownership of your copyrighted images can not.

Shooting for Stock

Travel pictures are used in magazines, newspapers, brochures, slide shows, calendars, and posters. In marketing stock photography the trick is to get the right picture to the right editor at the right time. This can be done through a picture agency or by direct contact with picture editors and art directors. Marketing travel pictures is not easy, but if you have talent, patience, and perseverance, it is worth the effort.

For example, consider some of our experiences. We once went to Tahiti on a shoot, were caught in a typhoon, and decided the trip was a washout in more ways than one. During the typhoon, we stepped out of our hotel room to take a few shots of the storm blowing the tops of the palm trees. A few years later, a one-time use of one of those slides was sold through our picture agency in Tokyo to Nissan, Inc. for $9,000. A sunset on the beach at Caneel Bay Plantation on St. John Island was used by a land-development company for $4,000. One of our shots of hot-air balloons appeared on a series of textbooks for $4,500. We negotiated a picture of a school girl in China for multiple use on textbook covers for $4,000. A picture of Sugar Loaf Mountain in Rio de Janeiro was used by Pan-American Airline for $1,000. These were all good pictures, but not ones we particularly consider our best. More routine sales for stock use range from $100 to $500.

Don't restrict yourself to shooting only faraway or exotic places for stock. Photograph the normal scenes around you; they sell well, too. Capture people reacting to and communicating with each other, and focus on mixed generations: grand-

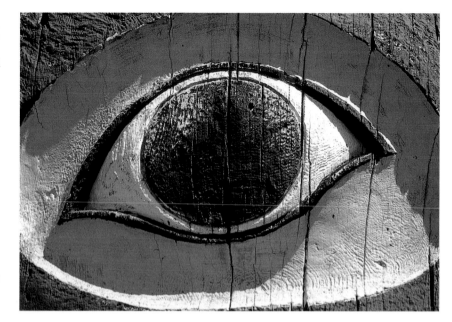

Isolate clean, graphic images when taking pictures for stock. The top detail of an eye happens to be from a totem pole in Sitka, Alaska, but the picture could be used in a totally different context.

We caught this smiling schoolgirl on a playground in China. A tight vertical crop of her face and hands appeared on the covers of a series of United States textbooks, which netted us over $4,000.

children with grandparents, mothers and sons, and fathers and daughters. Photograph people with animals. Pictures of all these subjects are potentially big earners. Not only will they pay for themselves, someday they may also pay for the monthly payments on your new house.

When shooting for stock, always use 35mm color-transparency film. Editors looking for pictures prefer to use transparency film for reproduction. You can always have black-and-white glossy prints made from color slides by having black-and-white inter-negatives made at a local custom film-processing lab.

While you are taking travel pictures, keep in mind what might sell. Generic pictures of beaches and sunsets are always good subjects. Action shots of wind surfers, tennis players, and golfers make good stock images. When shooting in a city, look for scenes that symbolize its identity and avoid obscure scenes that aren't readily recognizable. For example, when you are in Washington, D.C., shoot the Capitol Building and the White House. We have a routine picture of the White House, shot through the fence from the sidewalk, that was used by a magazine for $400. Almost everyone who visits Washington with a camera takes this picture, but we had it on the editor's desk when he needed it.

Edit your slides carefully and keep only those photographs you are willing to have attributed to you. Put caption information and your copyright on the slide mounts. This can be done neatly with a pen directly on the mount, or the information can be typed on gummed labels that are transferred to the slide. The copyright symbol, which should read © your name and the year the picture was taken—for example, © Carl Purcell 1988—can be made up on a rubber stamp that shouldn't be larger than the narrow side of a slide mount. We do our captions on gummed labels produced by our computer and a dot-matrix printer.

Filing Your Slides
The next step is to categorize and file your slides in an organized

Slides must be carefully edited and captioned before filing.

fashion. Photographers arrive home from their travels with memorable images but frequently give no thought to putting their pictures into an accessible order. Color slides usually come back from the processing lab in little yellow boxes. A typical reaction is to write the shoot's geographic location on the outside of the box and put it on a closet shelf with other yellow boxes.

When you're dealing with less than twenty-five boxes, storing slides in their original boxes is a reasonable approach. However, being a photographer can be compared to being the Sorcerer's Apprentice; within a few years you'll be flooded by a river of yellow boxes. Soon you'll find it impossible to locate that stunning color slide of the Taj Mahal at sunset or that action shot of a surfer in Hawaii. Like everything else of value in life, photographs can and should be organized and filed in a logical way.

In an effort to get organized some photographers have turned to plastic slide pages for filing their color slides. These pages are usually translucent on one side and transparent on the other and are designed to hold twenty slides in individual pockets. They can be held up to a light source or placed on a light table to review the images and can be stored in file cabinets or loose-leaf ring binders. Some slide pages are composed of polyvinyl chloride, a material that causes an adverse chemical reaction with color-transparency emulsions over a period of time. When buying slide pages, check the specifications on the package to see whether polyvinyl chloride has been used. If so, ask for

archival sleeves, designed for permanently filing slides, that are not made from polyvinyl chloride.

Also watch moisture retention and the danger of fungus or mildew when filing slides in plastic sleeves. A closed plastic pocket traps any moisture present when a slide is inserted in a sleeve, and this can be potentially damaging to the image. None of this negates the value of using plastic slide pages for temporary storage, mailing, or submission to editors and art directors, or even for storing a small collection of slides, not exceeding a few thousand images. Indeed, slide sleeves are the preferred way to mail transparencies, and they facilitate quick review on a light table.

We prefer a simple file-drawer system which can vary from custom-made drawers to modified kitchen or hardware cabinets. Basically, what you need is a shallow drawer filled with channels that are the exact width of a 35mm color slide. Thousands of slides can be filed in a single such drawer and categorized according to subject by tabs that stick up for identification. Such a file should be kept in an air-conditioned room that is never subject to extreme temperatures and where the humidity is kept at a minimum.

We have used two such drawer systems. For years we used made-to-order individual wooden drawers, but now we are using metal cabinets that each contain five metal drawers and are manufactured by Neumade Products, 200 Connecticut Avenue, Norwalk, Connecticut 06856. Both the wooden and metal systems are highly satisfactory, but the metal cabinets are more durable and discourage insects. Although many camera stores don't carry them, the Neumade SF-5-S file drawers can usually be ordered through large photography-supply stores.

Some of the most sophisticated slide storage and filing systems are available from Abodia, Elden Enterprises, Inc., P.O. Box 3201, Charleston, WV 25332. These systems incorporate vertical slide racks in well-constructed cabinets that feature balanced fluorescent light sources. These racks are especially

helpful for arranging slides in a particular sequence for a slide-show presentation or for seeing and comparing all your slides on a specific subject.

The subject of picture organization is critical to travel photographers who need easy access to their files in order to market their work. It is natural for travel photographers to file their pictures according to geographic categories. Our file is broken down alphabetically, first by continent, then by country, then by cities or regions, and then by subject headings such as hotels, marketplaces, people, and street scenes. For example, under Cairo, Egypt, three categories might be: "Cairo–papyrus," "Cairo–people," and "Cairo–pyramids."

If your photographic interest is a particular subject, such as sports, you might prefer to file your slides in main categories such as "Soccer," "Swimming," and "Surfing" and then use locations as subheadings, for example: "Swimming-Nashville," "Swimming-New Orleans," "Swimming-Norfolk." A separate "miscellaneous" file is good for holding generic slides that you don't choose to put in geographic categories. For example, it might not be clear whether a cloud is in Africa or Indiana, but you should want to know whether it is a cirrus or cumulus, so you should label it accordingly and file it under "Miscellaneous-Clouds."

You must make these filing decisions on the basis of your own specialties and interests. Your choice of system will depend on your needs and the number of slides to be filed. Don't wait any longer to start labeling and filing your slides in some organized manner. You can't sell the publication rights to a slide if you can't find it when you need it. Keep those slides in their place!

When your slide file is organized, make a complete list of all your categories, and from this list com-

This photo of a windsurfer in Fort Lauderdale, Florida, shows how color can be used as the focal point in a picture.

pose an attractive index that is easy to read and use. This can be simply typed and photocopied or you can have it done by a local print shop. This index will be useful to you, and it is also a useful marketing tool to send to photography editors, art directors, and picture agencies.

Going Freelance

People often ask us, "When should we start freelancing full time? How do we get started?" Unfortunately, some of these inquiries have come from people who said that they were interested in photography, had already quit their jobs, and wanted information about getting started as photographers. We cannot stress the following rule strongly enough: Don't quit your job until you are making at least one-half your total income from doing on-the-side freelancing!

A second rule is also important: Use the assistance and advice of lawyers and accountants in your area for the final wording of all contracts and tax returns. We are neither lawyers nor accountants and can suggest only rough guidelines for you to refer to in evolving your own business. Your best resources for help in developing copyrights, submission forms, model releases, and invoices are the two ASMP books described earlier. They are indispensable business guides for freelance photographers.

After you've set up usable slide files and categorized them for easy retrieval, you are ready to establish client files for correspondence so that you can keep records of slide submissions and returns. Information on each client should include the name of the publication; its address; your contact's name, title, and telephone number; the date the slides were sent and their subject; how many slides were sent; how many were returned and when; how many slides the client kept; how many were published and in what size; and the amount you were paid.

Any slides that you send out for any reason should be accompanied by a submission form that lists: the date; your name and address; your contact's name and address and the

publication or firm name; and a description of the pictures sent, their format, and their number. It should also state that the slides are copyrighted by you and that there is a liability for loss or damage to any original slide of fifteen-hundred dollars. (Some photographers and photography buyers prefer to deal exclusively with duplicate slides, but if you are sending out great numbers of slides for review, the cost of making dupes can be prohibitive.) Your submissions form should also include a statement of your research and holding fees. We allow a thirty-day holding period, after which we charge a one-dollar holding fee per slide per day unless prior arrangements for a longer holding period were made with us. We rarely charge a research fee unless the picture request is unusually long and involved and then only if our subsequent research does not result in a sale. Some submission forms also include a clause about disputes between you and your clients such that in cases of liability or infringement, all attorney-and-court costs will be paid by your client.

You should also keep files on business expenses and income. If you are running your freelance business from your home, measure the exact amount of living space in your house. Then measure the exact amount of space used by your business. The percentage of space used by your business is the percentage of your rent-and-utilities costs that may be tax deductible, depending on state tax laws. Keep a meticulous account of the following business expenses: taxes (you must register your business in your county); postage; office supplies, such as paper, letterheads, and slide pages; photographic equipment; office furniture and equipment, such as filing and slide cabinets; telephone bills (separate your business-related and your personal calls and costs); your travel costs for shooting photographs; office help (your spouse counts only if he or she doesn't co-own the business); entertainment that is strictly business related, subscription fees for business-related professional organizations; office rent if you have

The young boy feeding sea gulls in Key Largo is another example of a good, solid, stock shot. The boy's arm and the gulls' wings make a clean graphic design against the sky. The photograph works better as a stock shot because you don't see the boy's face.

Sometimes the best sellers in your stock file are just background photos on which advertising copy can be superimposed. This sunset shot of the Masai Mara plain in East Africa is enhanced by the "fingers of God" effect of the light spilling down from the clouds.

an office away from home; maintenance and repair of your camera equipment; film and processing; and any brochures, advertising, or flyers for publicity.

When you know what pictures are going to be used from a submission, you will usually have to send an invoice before the publication will pay you. Refer to the fee guidelines suggested by the *ASMP Stock Photography Handbook*. The normal procedure for a second, identical use of a photograph (for example, one that appears in a reprint of a textbook or brochure) is to charge one-half the fee paid for the first-time use. Although the ASMP rates are considered standard, your clients may wish to bargain according to the limitations of their budgets. You should be slightly flexible, but don't undersell your work. No one will consider your photography to be of any value if you, the photographer, don't value it. It is a fatal mistake to give away work in hopes of having it published. The end result will simply be that editors know you consider your work to be worthless.

Keeping a tear-sheets file of your published photographs can be extremely helpful to you and should be updated meticulously. Once you have started to sell your pictures on a regular basis and have established your name, you should maintain a portfolio of tear sheets to show potential clients, and you might consider having a folder or brochure displaying samples of your work printed. A four-color brochure can be very expensive. One way to get a color folder free, or at least at a very low cost, is to sell a spread of color pictures to a high-quality magazine and ask the editor to have a quantity of color signatures run off for your personal use. Sometimes the editors will do this at no charge, but even if you must pay, the cost is very reasonable. These color signatures can be mailed to potential clients with your slide index, and soon you may have editors calling or writing when they are looking for subjects on your list.

You've heard of being "land poor?" Well, don't be "equipment poor!" Buy only the equipment you need for everyday use. If you do unusual jobs that require special equipment, rent it. Before you pull out your wallet, ask yourself, "Will I make more money because I own this equipment?" If the answer is "No," don't spend the money.

Marketing Your Work

One of the best pieces of advice we can give you is to diversify. It is possible for you to make money with your photographs in several ways: 1) through stock agencies; 2) by marketing stock from your own home or office; 3) by submitting your pictures with articles written by yourself or with the help of a writer-friend; 4) through assignments; 5) selling prints; and 6) giving slide-show lectures. Although any of these markets can provide a substantial amount of money, it is better for you to tap as many outlets for sales as possible. For example, compare what would happen if you attempt to sell photographs to newspapers without text to what would happen if you submit an article with photographs. Although it is possible you'll make a few sales of pictures alone to newspapers needing pictures for current articles, you are far more likely to make a sale if you offer a complete package, including an article and photographs to illustrate it.

Obviously, the ability to write clearly and concisely can be very helpful in marketing your pictures. You must be able to express yourself clearly on paper in order to communicate ideas when submitting queries to editors. Pictures need to be captioned, but writing well is even more important when combining text with pictures. This type of package is very appealing to an editor because it is ready to publish without additional work. If you are strictly a photographer without any talent as a writer, it may be to your advantage to team up with a writer. Such a partnership can be professionally beneficial to both parties. The more you diversify, the more money you'll make.

Most discount bookstores carry *Photographers Market*, a hardbound book, updated yearly, containing the names, addresses, and photography needs of the world's leading picture buyers. Read the book carefully and note the names of those art directors who buy the kind of photographs you shoot. Send these people copies of your slide index so that they'll have it in their photo research files when they're looking for pictures.

If you want to send a sample of your work with the index, don't expect to have it returned. The simplest way to circulate samples of your work is to have a small selection of high-quality dupes made. Never, never send unsolicited original slides in the mail. If you send a self-addressed stamped envelope with your duplicate slides, you might get them back, but art directors cannot and will not assume responsibility for material they didn't ask to see.

Subscribe to a photo-request newsletter. If you have a computer, there are several computer networks that broadcast requests for photographs. The best of these are *Photobulletin*, Route 2, Box 93, Osceola, Wisconsin 54020, which also sends out its transmissions by mail if you don't have a computer, and *Vertical Market Services, Inc.*, 1001 South Bayshore Drive, Miami, Florida 33131.

Query editors about story or photography ideas that you have. First, make sure you know the publication. Buy an issue or two. You would obviously not query a magazine for senior citizens about an article on a parachutist who is twelve years old. If you're focusing on newspapers, you should have a current *Editor & Publisher Yearbook* on hand for your queries. You can find it at your local library or write to Editor & Publisher, 11 West 19th Street, New York, New York 10011. Having this reference will help you personalize your cover letters by addressing travel or feature editors by name.

Stock Agencies

Photographers Market is a good source for finding the names of picture agencies where you might want to place your slides. Before you send your work to an agency, write or call first to verify that they want to review your slides. If they show interest, send them about three hundred of your very best slides with a cover letter and enclose return postage. To be sure that you are a serious, producing photographer, some agencies will want to review another shipment of more pictures before signing a contract with you. Many picture agencies request an exclusive contract with a new photographer, but we recommend that you hold out for a nonexclusive arrangement.

Generally, it is easier to allow an agency to handle your stock sales than to pursue these sales yourself, and it is well worth it to give an agency the usual fifty-percent commission for their sales of your work. Expect to wait at least one year after you have sent your first batch of slides to an agency before you start making money from them. It is safe to estimate that you'll make approximately one dollar per year per slide for every slide kept in agency files.

Selling Prints

Travel pictures can also be matted and framed and sold at art shows, galleries, and county fairs. It is important to achieve good quality in the color printing and framing, but if you can do the printing and framing yourself, it will save money and provide you with a larger margin of profit. Our advice is to determine the retail outlets for your framed pictures in advance and decide if you can devote enough time to selling them at a county or craft fair or if you should assign the marketing to an established gallery or framing shop.

The first step, of course, is having the enlargements made. Amateur photographers are sometimes at a loss as to where to have this done. Your hometown photo dealer probably sends some of the film processing and printing to a local lab where the quality of the color prints varies. Some local labs are not equipped to make prints larger than 11×14. When you need a very special enlargement, your best bet is to have it done by a custom lab.

Some skilled photographers make

their own prints. These fall into two categories: prints made from color negatives or internegatives, and Cibachrome prints made directly from slides. If you don't have a custom lab in your hometown, there are some labs where you can order custom prints by mail. We like Jet Color Lab in Seattle, Washington. You can get their literature and price lists by writing Mike Tutty, P.O. Box 9777, Seattle, Washington, 98109.

An alternative is to have a 20 × 30 poster print made by Eastman Kodak. This is not a custom print (no cropping is permitted), but the quality is excellent, and if you aren't satisfied with the results, Kodak will remake the print at no cost. Orders can be placed through your local camera store.

The next step is to have your picture framed or mounted. You are faced with a multitude of choices concerning frames, mattes, dry mounting, and glass, and you also must decide whether to have this done professionally or do it yourself. We should point out that proper framing or mounting can cost much more than the print itself. Sometimes, after trial and error, you can find an innovative, moderately priced framer. For some of our favorite photographs, the framing shop we found (Snow Goose Gallery, 5223 Wisconsin Avenue, Washington, D.C., 20015) neatly insets a metal plate, inscribed with the title and the photographer's name, into the matte.

If you must do it yourself, our advice is to avoid buying a ready-made-frame and trying to do it at home. Many framing shops will provide instruction on framing on the premises as long as you buy the materials from them. They have a wide selection of mattes and frames plus the necessary equipment for dry mounting.

There are many different styles of frames and types of mattes, and there is even a difference in glass. One of the most popular frames for photographs is the silver-metal museum frame. It is simple, classic, and does nothing to distract from the picture itself. This is very appropriate for modern images with clean graphic elements and also works very well with abstract photographs. With more traditional subjects you might want a frame made of wood.

We interviewed one of the experts at the Snow Goose Gallery to find out what rules they follow when framing photographs. Most photographs don't require archival framing (in which acid-free mattes and backings are used), but should be dry mounted for maximum stability and a smooth surface. When glass or Plexiglas is used, the surface shouldn't be in direct contact with the photograph because this can cause moisture to condense between the glass and the picture. Most nonglare glass will make a photograph appear less sharp. Standard glass is very acceptable, but it has the disadvantage of reflecting light from some angles. Usually Denglas, a very thin, relatively expensive material, can reduce distracting reflection.

A collectors print, such as a numbered Ansel Adams or Edward Weston, shouldn't be dry mounted since this process will destroy or reduce its commercial value. Such a print should never be hung in the direct sunlight; this rule applies to any photographic print.

Although we have several nicely framed photographs, most of our large prints are box mounted or float mounted when we put them on exhibit or display them in our offices. In some cases, we have done the mounting ourselves with PPC Box Frames made in Shadyside, Maryland. These box frames have 1½-inch deep sides available in various colors and wood grains. The surface is covered with a protective wax-paper sheet that can be peeled off to expose the pressure-sensitive adhesive just before the photographic print is affixed. Pressure is applied with a roller to make sure the print is smoothly attached to the box mount. A sharp razor blade or X-acto knife is used to trim the print so that it is flush with the mount. Mounting and trimming with box mounts is not difficult, but the company is willing to mount the prints for you at no additional cost if you send the prints to them.

Producing a Slide Show

Another source of possible income from your travel pictures is the slide show. Whether you do one for pleasure or profit, it should be done with the highest professional standards. Some of our photography colleagues make a substantial living from producing slide shows for travel clients or just presenting illustrated lectures on travel destinations.

The golden rule for putting on a slide show is "don't bore your audience," but many amateur photographers do just that. There are some basic guidelines for both simple slide shows and more sophisticated presentations. Follow them and you'll hold the attention of your audience and get your message across.

First, you'll need a projector. We often avoid recommending specific pieces of photographic equipment, but in the case of slide projectors, there are compelling reasons for us to make an exception. The Kodak Carousel has been the work horse of the audiovisual industry for many years, and it is highly suitable and dependable for producing a slide show. Among its features are a standard eighty-slide-capacity tray, a zoom lens, and a remote-control cord for advancing and focusing. Probably ninety percent of the amateur and audiovisual market has been cornered by the Kodak Carousel. This projector utilizes a circular horizontal tray that rotates like a merry-go-round, dropping each slide into the projector slot by gravity feed. We personally use Carousel projectors and have chosen models with the autofocus feature and curved-field zoom lenses that work very well with cardboard-mounted slides. The zoom lens allows you to adjust your projector to screen distance according to the size of the room and the number of people in your audience. Two other companies making slide projectors are Leitz and Elmo.

For projecting your show, the projector should be on a solid table about four and a half feet high. Allow at least fifteen feet from your screen to the first person in the front row of your audience. You can

cheat just a little in a small room. Adjust the image to a comfortable size with your zoom lens and you're ready to go.

Slide shows can be produced at several levels of sophistication. The simplest form is live narration with one tray of eighty slides and a remote extension cord. Some trays will hold 140 slides, but the slots are very narrow and may jam if the slide mounts are even slightly bent. The two most important things to remember are to keep your slide shows short, and to limit the screen time for each slide to an average of five seconds. Nothing is more tedious than to have to look at a slide for more than a minute while the narrator digresses on some unrelated subject. An eighty-slide show projected at an average of five seconds per slide will take about seven minutes. If you have a cassette tape recorder with a decent amplifier and speaker, you can add a musical background behind your narration.

A more complex approach might be to utilize two projectors and a dissolve unit. Dissolving from one image to another on a single screen makes a very pleasing transition. (If you don't have two projectors, Spiratone has an Auto-Fade device for use with a single slide projector that lets one slide fade out and the next one fade in without abrupt changes. You can write Spiratone at 135-06 Northern Boulevard, Flushing, New York, 11354-4063.)

Getting even more sophisticated, you can automatically program a whole show with a programming device and a cassette recorder by inserting the program cues on the tape with an inaudible signal. (Kodak makes an inexpensive programmer called the Kodak EC sound/slide synchronizer.) When played back through the programmer, this signal automatically advances the projector to the next slide. Such a show can be further polished by adding music to the sound track.

These two pictures are a part of our slide show on the Albuquerque Hot-Air Balloon Fiesta, the most photographed annual event in the United States.

What types of slides do you select for a slide show? Obviously they should be well-composed pictures, preferably with bright colors. The first task is to organize them according to categories, so that one flows logically into the next. Jot down a few lines of narration to help make visual transitions. Be ruthless in eliminating repetitious or superfluous pictures. Don't even consider those that don't meet your highest standards of photographic excellence.

For a travel show it is important to establish a sense of place. How do you let your viewers know that the sidewalk café is in France? The green umbrellas advertise "Perrier" and the bread basket is filled with those distinctive loaves, not to mention the gentleman wearing a beret. You can organize your slides chronologically on the thesis that "today is Tuesday, so it must be Belgium," or you can organize them by subject. You might have ten slides on the French Riviera, eight slides on the Loire Valley, and eleven slides on Brittany.

Your choice of slides is very important in establishing the setting and can be used to make a point. One example is to visually indicate the end of the show. One woman ended her slide show about her safari to Africa with a sunset shot of Mount Kilamanjaro featuring, in the foreground, the rear end of a zebra. We ended a slide presentation on an air show and balloon fiesta with a stunt plane nose diving toward the ground.

There are a few simple rules for producing any type of slide show:

• Think about your slide show while taking your pictures. With vacation slides this can be chronologically based on the itinerary of your trip or even be thematic. The latter might deal with various aspects of a city such as statues, fountains, museums, or traffic.

• Move your slides quickly. Photographers often fall in love with their pictures and tend to keep them on the screen too long. A good rule of thumb is never to show a slide longer than five seconds. Just remember how quickly, by choice, you leaf through a picture book.

• Keep your show short. Fifteen minutes is usually too long, ten minutes is better, and seven minutes is best. Two short slide shows are better than one long one. It is more effective to end the show with your audience wanting to see more than leaving them with the feeling that they've seen too much.

• Vary your images with closeups, medium shots, and scenics.

• Use people in your pictures for human interest.

• Use color to your advantage. Try bright colors for impact, subtle colors and monotones for mood.

• Don't use an original slide in a slide show if you are going to project it more than a few seconds or more than once. When you know which slides are going to be used in the slide show, have duplicates made of them. Slides fade under long exposure to bright light.

• Always rehearse a show with your equipment just before presenting it to an audience. Nothing is more frustrating than a malfunction before or during a slide show.

A script can be extremely helpful for either live or recorded slide shows. Be sparse with words and let the slides carry your message. Don't feel it is necessary to talk about every slide. It is better to give a prologue to your show, or to wait until the end for questions, than to give long verbal descriptions that interfere with your visual presentation. If the image is self-explanatory, let it stand on its own. Often you can show a whole series of slides with nothing but music behind them.

Limiting your slide show to seven minutes is a test of discipline, since most people who have taken a trip are eager to show every image they took. Trust us when we say your audience will enjoy the seven minute show far more than a full hour of slides. In order to prepare a longer performance, you'll have the difficult task of maintaining the excitement and fast-moving pace. For this, you must have an unusually large file of exceptionally good slides on your subject. If you have been asked to give an hour or more presentation, it is advisable to give a talk first, followed by a fifteen-minute slide show, followed by another explanatory talk and then, perhaps, closing with a final short slide show.

If you prefer a written introductory or closing title slide, there are a few companies that can burn titles on your slides or sell you lead-and-end title slides. To get a catalog from one such company, write Donars Productions, P.O. Box 24, Loveland, Colorado, 80539. This company is also able to combine several slides in one to form a composite slide. For specific kinds of slide shows, composite slides may be useful, as in a before-and-after comparison or to show similarity and difference.

When the show is all together and your equipment is running smoothly, pass the popcorn and turn out the lights. Good pictures and good pacing will keep them awake in the back row.

Keep Shooting!

Keep shooting! It takes building a comprehensive stock file and years of filling stock requests accurately and promptly before your photographs will make enough money for you to buy fancy cars. Getting started and becoming successful at marketing your photographs is a long and difficult procedure, but after you've established a sizeable file and have made the right contacts with picture editors and buyers, being a freelance photographer can be profitable. In the meantime, as you shoot outstanding pictures, put those photographs to work and keep taking more!

Index

SPACE, STARS, AND THE BEGINNING OF TIME

WHAT THE HUBBLE TELESCOPE SAW

ELAINE SCOTT

HOUGHTON MIFFLIN HARCOURT › BOSTON NEW YORK

The text was set in 13-point Scala.
Book design by Sharismar Rodriguez

▶ LIBRARY OF CONGRESS CATALOGING-
IN-PUBLICATION CATALOGED THE HARDCOVER
EDITION AS FOLLOWS:
Library of Congress Cataloging-in-Publication Data
Scott, Elaine, 1940–Space, stars, and the beginning of time :
what the Hubble telescope saw / by Elaine Scott.p. cm.1. Hubble Space
Telescope (Spacecraft)—Juvenile literature. I. Title. QB500.268.S364
2011522'.2919—dc222010008040
ISBN: 978-0-547-24189-0 hardcover
ISBN: 978-1-328-89577-6 paperback
Manufactured in China
SCP 10 9 8 7 6 5 4 3 2 1
4500705500

Front cover: Two galaxies collide in this spectacular Hubble image,
resulting in the birth of billions of stars. NASA/ESA and the Hubble
Heritage Team (STScI/AURA) **Back cover:** The newly repaired and
updated Hubble Telescope. NASA

Title page: The Hubble reveals galaxy NGC1672, more than 60,000
million light-years away from Earth. Star-forming clouds and dark
bands of interstellar dust appear along the edges of the galaxy's spiral
arms. NASA, ESA, and the Hubble Heritage Team (STScI/AURA)—
ESA/Hubble Collaboration

Contents page: The gorgeous, winding arms of galaxy NGC5194 are
actually long lanes of stars and gas laced with dust. The galaxy's
face-on view allows astronomers to use Hubble images to study this
classic spiral galaxy's structure and star formation processes. To the far
right is another galaxy, NGC5195. NASA, ESA, and the Hubble Heritage
Team (STScI/AURA)—ESA/Hubble Collaboration

ACKNOWLEDGMENTS

No book is ever written by the author alone, and this one is no exception. I want to thank my
editor, Jennifer Greene, whose wise queries made this a far better manuscript than it might
have been without them. Zolt Levay of the Space Telescope Science Institute was wonderfully
helpful with the picture research and Cheryl Gundy, also of STScI, has been a steady support as
I have written all my books on space and the Hubble. Dr. Laura Danley graciously answered my
questions years ago, and now as well. I'm saving the last accolade for Dr. Mario Livio, senior
astrophysicist at STScI. I continue to be stunned that this brilliant, distinguished scholar took
time from his demanding schedule to read the manuscript and correct the errors he found.

I am deeply grateful to all of you.
—E.S.

CONTENTS

INTRODUCTION

HAVE YOU EVER wished you could travel back in time? Or visit another planet? Or see a star close up? Have you ever wondered about the mysteries of the universe, and whether other life-forms, similar to humans, exist somewhere? These are important questions that people have been asking for hundreds of years. Throughout those years many books—fact and fiction—have been written as authors and readers seek answers to the questions they have.

Perhaps one of the most beloved tales about travel to distant galaxies is Madeleine L'Engle's novel *A Wrinkle in Time*. It tells the story of Meg Murry, her little brother, Charles Wallace, and their friend Calvin, who go on a mysterious journey through the universe in search of the Murry children's father, who has vanished from planet Earth. When Mrs. Murry tries to explain Mr. Murry's sudden disappearance, Meg asks her mother, "Do you think things always have an explanation?"

Mrs. Murry replies that she believes they do, but goes on to say,

"With our human limitations, we're not always able to understand the explanations. But you see, Meg, just because we don't understand doesn't mean that the explanation doesn't exist."

Meg answers, "I like to understand things."

Like Meg, many of us want to understand things, even if the topics are difficult ones—like space, time, and the mysteries of the universe. To understand anything we must ask questions. Madeleine L'Engle was no exception; she liked to ask questions, too. In her introduction to *A Wrinkle in Time,* she asks her readers: "If anyone invited you to go to a newly discovered galaxy, would you go?" How would you answer? *Would* you go? Would you be frightened? Excited? Curious? Without the aid of a telescope, you can look up into the night sky and see a few of the planets in our solar system and thousands of stars. With a telescope, we are able to see billions of stars, and astronomers have detected hundreds of planets orbiting in solar systems beyond our own. Many wonder, is Earth *really* the only planet that supports life? What do you think other planets would be like?

Madeleine L'Engle used fiction—made-up characters and a made-up story—to explore important questions about the universe. Occasionally a novel, such as *A Wrinkle in Time,* becomes meaningful for generations of readers. Likewise, a scientific instrument can become so important, so useful, its contributions to science so amazing, that it changes the way people look at themselves and their world. The Hubble Space Telescope is that kind of instrument. It has changed the way we understand the universe and Earth's place in it.

Named for the great twentieth-century astronomer Edwin

The Hubble's instruments captured this image of a cloud of space dust and gas that surrounds a giant star at the outer edge of the Milky Way galaxy.
NASA AND THE HUBBLE HERITAGE TEAM (AURA/STSCI)

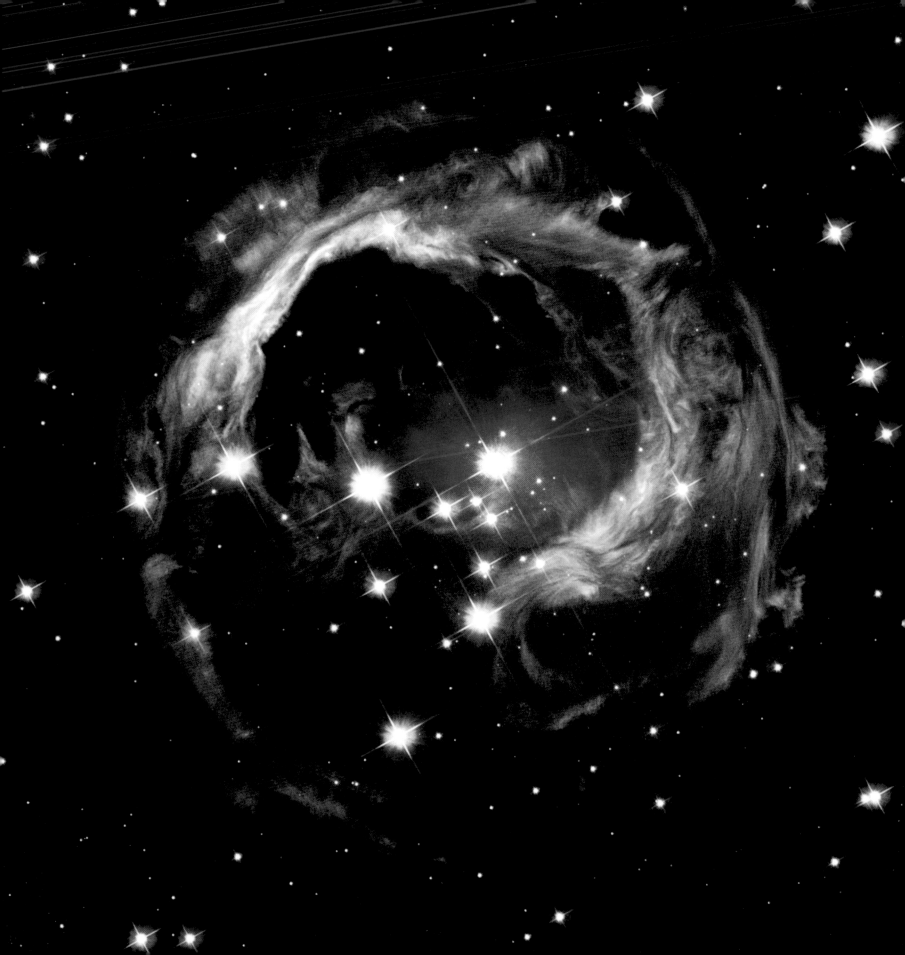

The Hubble Space Telescope orbits high above Earth's atmosphere, returning spectacular images of the universe to Earth. STScI

Hubble (1889–1953), the Hubble Space Telescope has been called one of the greatest scientific instruments of all time. The information it has returned to astronomers and other scientists around the world—each and every *week*—is enough to fill a 3,600-foot-long bookshelf. That's the length of ten football fields laid out end to end! Cameras onboard this great observatory photograph new stars as they are born, and old stars as they die. Images reveal massive black holes from which nothing, not even light, can escape. The Hubble has detected new planets orbiting other stars, proving that our solar system with its eight planets isn't the only solar system in the universe. Scientists have known about gravity, the force that attracts, or pulls, objects with mass toward each other, since Isaac Newton (1643–1727) first wrote about it. Recently, astronomers have used the Hubble to reveal another mystery, dark energy, which exerts a force that appears to be pulling things apart.

This remarkable telescope shows us not only what is happening in the universe now, but also what has happened in the past. The Hubble can retrieve data from billions of years ago, almost to the moment the universe was born in a massive explosion known as the Big Bang. Knowing what has happened in the past can help scientists determine what may happen in the future.

Like any instrument, the Hubble Space Telescope has needed maintenance throughout the years. Servicing the Hubble is dangerous and expensive work. However, during the time it has been in orbit, teams of spacewalking astronauts have competed for the privilege of making the trip to the space observatory. On May 11, 2009, a crew of seven astronauts launched into space from

Cape Canaveral to service the Hubble for the fifth and final time, improving its capabilities and making necessary repairs. Four of the astronauts would be the last human beings to touch the telescope.

As he anticipated the final mission to the Hubble, Mission Commander Scott Altman said, "Hubble puts cutting-edge science together with a visual image that grabs the public's imagination. I think that's the first step in exploration . . . it's like taking you on a journey thirteen and a half billion light-years away, while you sit there at home and look out at the universe."

Before the Hubble was launched, there were many things about space, time, and our universe that astronomers, physicists, and other scientists didn't understand. But just as Mrs. Murry told Meg, it didn't mean there were no explanations to be found. The great physicist Albert Einstein (1879–1955) once said, "The important thing is not to stop questioning." During the twenty years it has been in orbit, the Hubble Space Telescope has provided many explanations about questions scientists have had about the universe. Of course, for every question it has answered, it has raised more, which is not a bad thing. Scientists believe that explanations for the mysteries of the universe exist and, therefore, it is always possible to find answers. Dr. Laura Danly, an astrophysicist who worked with the Hubble Space Telescope and is now curator at the Griffith Observatory in Los Angeles, California, said, "It annoys me when people talk about 'the secrets of the universe.' The universe doesn't have secrets. It reveals itself to us." The Hubble Space Telescope helps us see what those revelations are.

Earth, Moon, and the Hubble. Galileo studied the Moon with his telescope, but he probably could not have imagined a telescope that would take pictures of the Moon from space. STS-103 CREW AND NASA

The Spyglass Grows Up

Hans Lippershey (LIP-er-shy) (1570–1619), a Dutch optician, is credited with the invention of the telescope in 1608. Lippershey held two lenses in front of each other and discovered that objects viewed through both lenses appear larger and closer than they actually are. Since it is inconvenient to hold a lens in each hand for any length of time, Lippershey mounted them on either end of a long tube, thus creating the telescope. Lippershey wanted the Dutch government to give him a pension in exchange for his telescope, but because there were a few other people who claimed the telescope as their invention, the government refused to give Lippershey either a pension or a patent. But the Dutch government did pay him 900 florins, roughly $360. In 1608, that was a large sum of money. The Dutch used the telescope to spy on enemy ships that approached by sea, so Lippershey's invention became known as a "spyglass." Once scientists began to use the instru-

The Hubble captured this display of starlight, glowing gas, and dark clouds of interstellar dust in Galaxy NGC 1300. Blue and red giant stars can be seen in its spiral arms.

NASA, ESA, and the Hubble Heritage Team (STScI)

A painting by Vincenzo Cesare Cantagalli showing Galileo dictating his observations to his secretary.

THE ART ARCHIVE/CORBIS

ment, however, it became obvious that it was useful for much more than spying.

Word of Lippershey's invention quickly spread through Europe. In Italy, a scientist named Galileo Galilei (ga-luh-LAY-oh ga-luh-LAY-ee) (1564–1642) learned of it and decided to make his own. In 1609, Galileo made a telescope that was superior to Lippershey's; it was able to magnify an object up to twenty times its size, while Lippershey's device only magnified objects up to three times. Galileo used his instrument differently, too. Instead of using it to look out to sea, Galileo turned his telescope upright to look at the heavens. He discovered—among many other things—that Jupiter had four moons, and that the Milky Way was not just a smear of light in the night sky, but rather was made up of billions of stars densely packed together.

The telescope also helped Galileo make his most controversial discovery. Based on observations made through his spyglass, Galileo concluded that Nicolaus Copernicus (Co-PER-ni-cus) (1473–1543) had been correct in stating that the Sun is at the center of our solar system, not the Earth, as most people in those days believed. Galileo hypothesized that the planets moved in a circular orbit around the Sun. It was not until years later that Johannes Kepler (1571–1601) would use a telescope to determine that the planets move around the sun in an oval, or elliptical, orbit.

Galileo's telescope revolutionized astronomy, but the instrument and others like it had an annoying flaw. The images astronomers saw through those early telescopes had colored edges. In 1668, the great English scientist Isaac Newton, who is best known for his work with gravity and the laws of motion, figured out how

Using his telescope, Galileo discovered that Jupiter has four moons, but he could not have seen Jupiter and its moon Ganymede as clearly as the Hubble did on April 9, 2007. NASA/ESA and E. Karkoschka (University of Arizona)

to fix the problem. Newton had been working with prisms, and he realized that the colored edge was caused by light being refracted, or bent, as it passed through a telescope's lenses. Newton built a telescope that used a mirror to *reflect* the light rather than refract it. The colored edge disappeared, and the images cleared up. Today, most telescopes use a combination of lenses and mirrors to capture light.

As years went by, more and more improvements were made to telescopes. But all telescopes, no matter how large or sophisticated, were Earth-bound, creating a difficulty that scientists couldn't improve by making further adjustments: astronomers still had to peer through Earth's atmosphere to view the night sky. Our atmosphere is made up of wiggling gases that hug our planet like the fuzz on a peach, and those gases can cause distortions in what the astronomers can see. Stars are often described as twinkling or dancing

Continued from page 8.

▶ **TESTING:** Hypotheses must be tested by other scientists before they can be accepted. Other astronomers repeated Galileo's observations and calculations. Most accepted Galileo's hypothesis that the planets traveled in a circular orbit around the Sun.

▶ **THEORY:** When many scientists agree on a hypothesis, it becomes a theory. Once a hypothesis becomes a theory, scientists begin to accept the theory as true. Galileo's hypothesis of planetary motion became a theory and was considered true. Kepler's discoveries disproved Galileo's theory. Kepler formed a new hypothesis: the planets move in elliptical orbits. When no one was able to disprove Kepler's hypothesis, it became a theory.

▶ **LAW:** Eventually theories can become scientific laws, like Isaac Newton's laws of motion. A law in science is a theory that has been carefully investigated and tested over many years and is widely accepted as fact. It is important to realize, however, that scientific theories and even laws can change when or if new information that disproves them becomes available, just as Kepler's discovery about the planets' elliptical orbits replaced Galileo's theory.

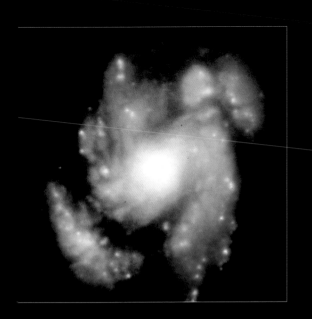

WIDE FIELD PLANETARY CAMERA 1

WIDE FIELD PLANETARY CAMERA 2

The defect in the Hubble's primary mirror, called a *spherical aberration*, made images appear out of focus and blurry. During the first servicing mission to the Hubble, astronauts installed a piece of new equipment called the Corrective Optics Space Telescope Axial Replacement, or COSTAR. Just as glasses fix out-of-focus vision in humans, COSTAR corrected the Wide Field Planetary Camera's fuzzy vision. Images show the core of galaxy M100 before the repair and after. STScI

(think "Twinkle, Twinkle, Little Star"), but in space, stars do not twinkle. They only twinkle if you see them from Earth. As long as scientists used telescopes on Earth, our planet's atmosphere would always be in the way.

The first astronomical satellite, Ariel 1, was launched by Great Britain in 1962. Telescopes had left Earth and moved to the sky. But these early satellites were small, and in most cases observed in only one wavelength of light. Then came the Hubble Space Telescope.

On April 24, 1990, the Hubble was carried into orbit. Unlike the previous satellites, the Hubble was a large instrument that would allow astronomers to observe in many different wavelengths of light. Scientists from around the world rejoiced at its launch. They eagerly anticipated what they might learn about our solar system and the universe as a whole.

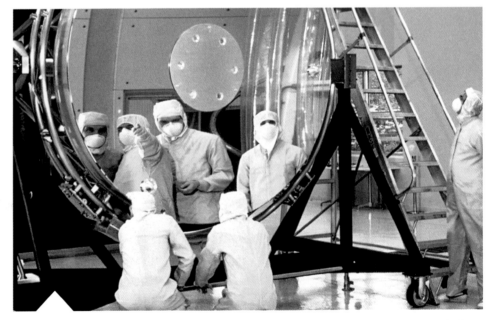

Before the Hubble's launch into space, technicians worked on its main mirror, which is eight feet in diameter. Light from an object enters the Hubble, reflects off this mirror, and hits a second, smaller mirror. The light then bounces back through a two-foot hole in the center of the main mirror where the Hubble's scientific instruments capture it. In this image, the hole is protected by a cover. The technicians are wearing masks and protective garments to prevent contamination of the telescope. NASA, 1990

The Hubble's cameras captured a star-forming region of space 210,000 light-years away, in a galaxy called the Small Magellanic Cloud. NASA/ESA AND A. NOTA (STScI/ESA)

INSTRUMENTS ONBOARD THE HUBBLE

▶ WIDE FIELD CAMERA 3 (WFC3):

This new camera will allow the Hubble to see deeper into space, and therefore farther back in time, than ever before. Light comes to us in different wavelengths. Young stars glow with ultraviolet light; but because the universe is expanding, the first stars and galaxies that formed after the birth of the universe are now so old and far away that their light is "redshifted," which means it only glows in the infrared wavelengths. This camera will be able to see and photograph ancient stars and galaxies that formed close to the beginning of time.

▶ COSMIC ORIGINS SPECTROGRAPH (COS):

A spectrograph is an optical instrument that studies objects that either absorb or produce light. The spectrograph can detect an object's electromagnetic spectrum, or the range of radiation it produces. The different types of radiation, from longest to shortest wave, include radio waves, microwaves, infrared light waves, visible light (the light we see), ultraviolet light, X-rays, and gamma rays, the shortest wavelength of all. The spectrograph works by breaking up light from an object into its individual wavelengths, so that the object's composition, temperature, motion, and other chemical and physical properties can be analyzed. The COS works mainly in the ultraviolet wavelength. Scientists will use this spectrograph to study how stars and galaxies formed and evolved over time. It will also help determine how some elements, like carbon and iron first came into being and have increased throughout the universe over time.

▶ SPACE TELESCOPE IMAGING SPECTROGRAPH (STIS):

Another spectrograph, this instrument was already installed on the Hubble, but needed repair. Before its failure in August 2004, STIS helped scientists discover and study supermassive black holes at the centers of other galaxies, and astronomers used it to analyze gases being blown off a very unstable star, Eta Carinae, that is in our galaxy.

The STIS is a general-purpose spectrograph that operates in the same way the COS does.

▶ ADVANCED CAMERA FOR SURVEYS (ACS):

Many of the Hubble's most amazing older images were taken with this camera, which suffered an electronic failure in January 2007. The camera was repaired on STS-125. The ACS will study large areas of the sky in both the visible and red wavelengths. Scientists will also use the ACS to unravel the mysteries of dark energy and dark matter.

▶ FINE GUIDANCE SENSOR (FGS):

This instrument locks on to a guide star, allowing the Hubble to remain precise and steady as it points toward an object.

▶ GYROSCOPES:

A gyroscope maintains direction and stability in moving objects such as planes, boats, and space telescopes. The Hubble has six gyroscopes and all six were replaced during the final mission. The FGS and gyroscopes give the Hubble the same level of precision as someone standing in Washington, D.C., with a laser beam, touching a dime someone else is holding in New York City!

▶ THE SCIENCE INSTRUMENT COMMAND & DATA HANDLING MODULE (SI C & DH):

SI C & DH is a computer and collection of electronic instruments that allows scientists on the ground to send commands to the Hubble in space. It also enables the telescope to send its information back to Earth.

▶ BATTERIES:

All of these instruments are powered by six batteries. The batteries receive their power from the telescope's two solar arrays, which gather energy from the Sun.

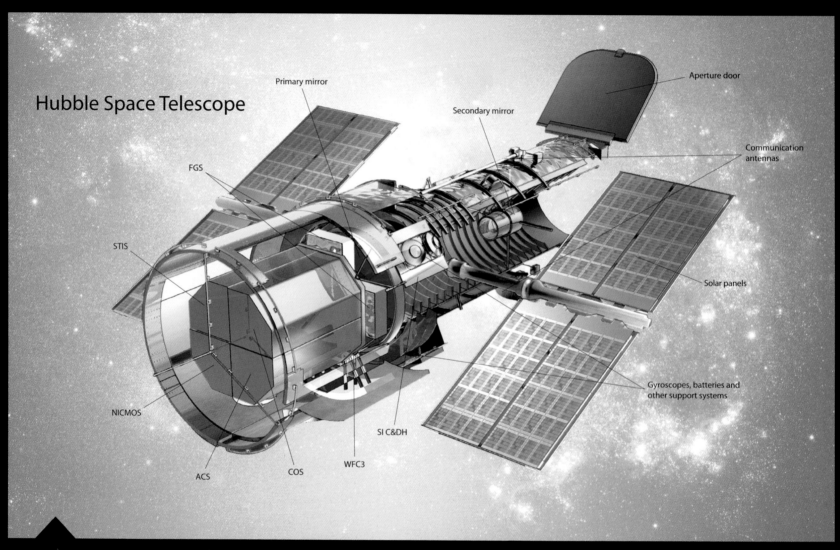

Hubble Space Telescope

- Primary mirror
- Secondary mirror
- Aperture door
- Communication antennas
- FGS
- STIS
- NICMOS
- ACS
- COS
- WFC3
- SI C&DH
- Solar panels
- Gyroscopes, batteries and other support systems

Instruments onboard the Hubble. Most of the Hubble's scientific instruments are located in the back third of the telescope. ESA

Light from the stars enters the telescope and is analyzed by its instruments. Then the data is sent to a relay satellite; from there the information goes to a ground station in White Sands, New Mexico, and on to Goddard Space Flight Center in Greenbelt, Maryland. The last stop for the data is the Space Telescope Science Institute in Baltimore, Maryland. STScI

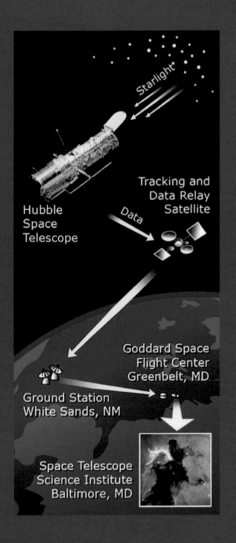

Starlight

Hubble Space Telescope

Data

Tracking and Data Relay Satellite

Goddard Space Flight Center Greenbelt, MD

Ground Station White Sands, NM

Space Telescope Science Institute Baltimore, MD

After all the excitement, the Hubble got off to a rocky start. The main mirror was ground incorrectly (by 1/50th of the thickness of a human hair!), so the telescope's ability to focus properly was severely limited. People who use eyeglasses can easily understand the Hubble's problem. A corrective lens in a pair of glasses or contact lenses focuses the light that comes through it, allowing the person wearing the lens to see clearly. If those lenses are incorrectly ground, the focus will be off and the person's vision will be blurry. In December 1993, the Hubble's vision problem was corrected during the first servicing mission to the telescope. Astronauts installed an instrument called the Corrective Optics Space Telescope Axial Replacement, or COSTAR for short. This instrument served as glasses for the Hubble, and soon thereafter, amazing images returned to Earth.

Astronauts have serviced the Hubble four more times since the first mission, installing new equipment and updating existing instruments each time. These missions are risky for the astronauts, they require years of training and planning, and each one costs hundreds of millions of dollars. However, the Hubble Space Telescope has allowed scientists to make discoveries about our universe that are, indeed, priceless, thanks to images that have been and continue to be shared around the world. According to the Space Telescope Science Institute, "The Hubble Space Telescope has had a major impact in every area of astronomy, from the solar system to objects at the edge of the universe."

TWO

A Final Visit to the Hubble

A LOT CAN GO wrong with a space flight—and many problems begin during launch. In 2003, the space shuttle *Columbia* was damaged during take off. As it ascended into space, debris struck and damaged part of the shuttle's heat shield. Nevertheless, the shuttle made it into orbit, and during the mission there weren't signs of serious problems. The astronauts onboard and Mission Control all thought things were going well. But *Columbia* had sustained damage beyond repair. The debris had torn a hole in a panel of the shuttle's left wing, so when *Columbia* made its fiery reentry into Earth's atmosphere, hot gases entered the wing and the shuttle broke up, killing all onboard. NASA immediately canceled all future shuttle missions while it investigated what had happened to *Columbia*. The final mission to the Hubble was among those canceled.

For a while, it looked as if the Hubble would never be serviced again. The observatory would be left in space, unrepaired—its use as a scientific instrument greatly lessened—and it would slowly fall apart. At the time, astronaut John Grunsfeld, who had made previous trips to the Hubble and had been scheduled to go on the final mission, said, "As a certified 'Hubble Hugger,' that hit me like a two-by-four. I just couldn't believe that we would prematurely make that decision."

He wasn't the only one who was disappointed. Scientists, students, teachers, and the general public cried out in protest. They could not imagine a world without the Hubble. At first, NASA stuck by its decision not to repair its famous telescope. Then the agency considered the possibility of sending robots to the Hubble instead of humans. But after careful consideration, that plan was laid aside. The telescope had been designed to be serviced by astronauts, not robots—astronauts who had trained for years to perform delicate work. Furthermore, some of the instruments onboard the Hubble had not been intended to be repaired at all, much less by robots. Captain Scott Altman saw additional value in sending astronauts on this mission. Astronauts would not only be more likely to successfully make the repairs the Hubble needed, they would also receive valuable training for future missions, when it will be important to make repairs in space. "I think it's a step that we need to take to make us better able to go to places like Mars," Altman said. "Being able to demonstrate this [repair] in space is a key element of us growing as a space-faring people."

Finally, in 2006, NASA announced that STS-125 would go forward. A crew of seven astronauts onboard *Atlantis* would head to the Hubble to service it one last time. John Grunsfeld, the "Hubble Hugger," would be the payload commander and make spacewalks

THE CREW

SCOTT ALTMAN, MISSION COMMANDER (D)

As mission commander Scott had overall responsibility for the safety and execution of the mission. He flew *Atlantis* to its rendezvous with the Hubble and was responsible for the operation of all the shuttle's systems. His duties included inspecting the heat shield for damage after the crew was in orbit.

GREGORY C. JOHNSON, PILOT (C)

In addition to piloting the shuttle, Gregory was the official photographer and charged with documenting the mission with an IMAX 3-D camera.

MICHAEL GOOD, MISSION SPECIALIST 1 (B)

Michael made the second and fourth spacewalks with Mike Massimino.

MEGAN MCARTHUR, MISSION SPECIALIST 2 (E)

Megan manipulated the robotic arm, getting the astronauts where they needed to be to service the telescope and performing other tasks.

JOHN GRUNSFELD, MISSION SPECIALIST 3 (F)

This was John's third trip to the Hubble and his fifth space flight. He was the lead spacewalker and conducted the first, third, and fifth spacewalks.

MIKE MASSIMINO, MISSION SPECIALIST 4 (A)

Mike made two spacewalks when the telescope was serviced in 2002, and two spacewalks with Michael Good on the final mission.

ANDREW "DREW" FEUSTEL, MISSION SPECIALIST 5 (G)

Drew performed the first, third, and fifth spacewalks with John Grunsfeld. This was his first space mission.

The crew of STS-125. The astronauts are wearing the training version of their orange launch and reentry garments. These pressure suits help astronauts withstand the stresses on their bodies as they break free of Earth's gravity on their launch into space, and as they feel its pull upon their return to Earth. **NASA**

Space shuttle *Atlantis* moments after its launch, carrying the crew of STS-125 to their rendezvous with the Hubble Space Telescope. **NASA**

with his partner Andrew Feustel. Mike Massimino and Michael Good would also make spacewalks. Megan McArthur would operate the robotic arm, and Gregory C. Johnson would pilot the shuttle. Scott Altman would lead them as mission commander.

Of course, the danger was still there. Even though NASA now understood what had happened to *Columbia,* something unexpected could always go wrong. But NASA had a plan to rescue the crew in the event of an emergency, and so the intense training began for the astronauts and for everyone on the ground who supports them.

It takes months, even years, to get one shuttle ready for a mission, but in an unprecedented move, NASA decided to prepare *two* shuttles for launch at Cape Canaveral. *Atlantis* would carry the crew to the Hubble, and *Endeavour* would be waiting on a nearby launch pad, ready to go, should the *Atlantis* crew need rescue.

On the fifth and final spacewalk of the mission, John Grunsfeld works on the Hubble. Note the yellow handrails that were installed all over the telescope in order to make it easier for astronauts to pull themselves around the observatory. A safety cable runs from Grunsfeld's right leg and is attached to a point on the shuttle, preventing him from floating away should he lose his grip on the handrail. **NASA**

Atlantis roared off the launch pad at 2:01 p.m. Eastern Daylight Time on May 11, 2009, as scheduled. Three days later, it caught up with the Hubble, which was orbiting Earth at 17,500 miles an hour. Once the shuttle and the Hubble were in the same orbit, Megan McArthur used the shuttle's robotic arm to capture the telescope and bring it safely to *Atlantis*'s cargo bay, the back portion of the space plane, open to space and used to carry equipment. Then in a series of five spacewalks that took place over five days, Drew Feustel, John Grunsfeld, Mike Massimino, and Michael Good began their work. In teams of two, the spacewalking astronauts installed Wide Field Camera 3, replaced all six of the Hubble's gyroscopes, installed the Cosmic Origins Spectrograph, and repaired the Advanced Camera for Surveys as well as the Space Telescope Imaging Spectrograph. Then they replaced batteries and sensors in order to keep the Hubble running for many years.

The space shuttle's robotic arm has two shoulder joints, one elbow joint, and three wrist joints and is 45 feet long. The arm is used to launch and retrieve satellites such as the Hubble and move astronauts around while they make spacewalks. It is also used in safety inspections. Sensors and cameras attached to the arm send information to the crew and to Mission Control, allowing experts to check the shuttle for any damage. **NASA**

On the outside, looking in. Michael Good peers through the window of *Atlantis* and greets crew members inside. Mike Massimino is in the background, on the left side of the shuttle's cargo bay. **NASA**

RESCUE IN SPACE

Most manned space flights go to the International Space Station, which is in continuous orbit around Earth. If a space shuttle was damaged, astronauts could take shelter there. But the Hubble Space Telescope is in orbit far away from the space station, and a crippled shuttle would not be able to make the journey there safely. Since it takes months, if not years, to get a shuttle ready to fly into space, and supplies onboard *Atlantis* support the crew of seven astronauts for three weeks, NASA prepared the shuttle *Endeavour,* too. Had something gone wrong with *Atlantis, Endeavour* and a reduced crew of four astronauts would have launched toward *Atlantis* within a week. Once *Endeavour* reached *Atlantis,* *Atlantis* would have used its robotic arm to latch on to *Endeavour.* With the two shuttles securely locked together, a series of spacewalks would have begun, and the seven-member crew from *Atlantis* would have slowly made its way to the safety of the replacement shuttle. With eleven astronauts onboard, *Endeavour* would have been a crowded shuttle as it made its way back to Earth!

Space shuttle *Atlantis* arrives at Edwards Air Force Base on May 24, 2009. Note the drag parachute on its tail, used to slow the vehicle down on the runway. The shuttle and its crew had made 197 orbits of Earth and traveled 5,276 million miles as the crew worked to repair the Hubble for the final time. NASA

Now that the job was complete, it was time for *Atlantis* to head back to Earth. Like all space shuttles, *Atlantis* is actually a space plane, complete with wings and landing gear. Although a shuttle is shot into space with a rocket, it returns to Earth as a powerless glider, rolling to a stop on a runway—usually at Cape Canaveral in Florida. Occasionally, the weather at Cape Canaveral makes it too dangerous for a shuttle to land there. In those cases, the spaceship can be rerouted to other landing sites in the United States or even other countries around the world. Because of potential storms in Florida, the crew had to remain in space for an extra two days, circling Earth. Finally, after making 197 orbits around Earth, covering 5,276 *million miles, Atlantis* and its crew landed safely at Edwards Air Force Base in California on May 24, 2009.

The mission was a complete success. The Hubble had been effectively serviced and repaired and was now capable of helping astronomers and cosmologists around the world explore deeper into space than ever before.

THE BEGINNING OF TIME

ASTRONOMY, one of the world's oldest sciences, is the observation and study of planets, stars, and galaxies. An astronomer is a scientist who practices astronomy. In a sense, the first humans were the first astronomers, since it is safe to assume they looked up into the night sky, gazing at the stars and the planets, surely wondering what they were. By 1300 B.C. the Chinese were recording their observations.

As time and science progressed, the field of astronomy grew, and other kinds of scientific study emerged, such as astrophysics. Astrophysics is concerned with the physics of the universe—its heat, light, and temperature, as well as the composition of stars, galaxies, and the interstellar medium (or the space between the stars and galaxies). An astrophysicist is a scientist who practices astrophysics.

Cosmology is the scientific study of the universe's origin, evolution, and ultimate fate. As a science, cosmology has existed

Albert Einstein in 1905, the year he published five papers, including his groundbreaking theory of relativity.
BETTMANN/CORBIS

for only approximately four hundred years. Following the invention of the telescope, astronomers, physicists, and other scientists have developed new theories that have been tested. While some theories have been disproved, others, such as Newton's laws of motion, have become scientific law. Occasionally, scientists will develop a theory and be surprised by the results of their own experiments. Allegedly, Albert Einstein did not believe his own theory of relativity, which suggested that our universe might be expanding. It took astronomer Edwin Hubble to prove to Einstein that his theory was correct.

Hubble arrived at the Mount Wilson Observatory in Pasadena, California, in 1919 to work with the Hooker Telescope, which was then the largest telescope in the world. At that time, most astronomers believed that the Milky Way was the only galaxy in the universe. During the period from 1922 to 1923, Edwin Hubble made observations with the Hooker Telescope and concluded that the faint smears of light people saw in the night sky were not clouds of gas, as astronomers had thought, but entire galaxies. Furthermore, Hubble proved that these galaxies were moving away, or *receding,* from one another. He also proved that the farther away galaxies were, the faster they were moving. In other words, Hubble showed that the universe is expanding at an astonishing rate.

Picture a deflated balloon with dots drawn so closely together they look like a single dot. Now fill the balloon with air and watch as the dots move away from one another. As with the dots on the inflated balloon, galaxies move away from one another. Of course, a balloon is finite—it has limits. Eventually, it will pop. The universe, on the other hand, could expand forever. Hubble's discovery is now called Hubble's law, and it ranks with other great discoveries, such as Newton's laws of motion and Einstein's theory of relativity. Edwin Hubble developed an equation that uses the speed of light to help calculate just how fast the universe is expanding. The measure of the rate of this expansion is called the Hubble Constant.

If the universe is expanding, then it follows that things must have been compacted at one time. In 1946, Roman Catholic priest, physicist, and astronomer Georges Lemaître (1894–1966), from Belgium, developed the Primeval Atom Hypothesis, the basis for the Big Bang theory, which says everything in the universe that ever was or will be—all matter and all energy—was compressed into a tiny point called a "singularity" or the "cosmic egg." According to Lemaître's hypothesis, which later became a theory, the cosmic egg was about the size of a grain of sand! It was hot and incredibly dense, because it contained all the building blocks of the universe. At some point this packed particle erupted in a fiery burst that created space and everything in it—our universe. This burst is called the Big Bang, the point at which the laws of physics began to apply to the universe.

The term Big Bang is a little misleading because it implies an explosion. A bomb explodes. When it does, matter from the bomb flies off into space that already exists. However, at the moment of the Big Bang, there was no space for anything to explode into. Space and everything else was still contained within the cosmic egg. At that moment, the cosmic egg did not explode *into* space; it erupted, *creating* space that continues to expand. Time as we understand it did not exist before the Big Bang, so scientists cannot explain what went on before it occurred. They can describe only what happened immediately following it in the first ten-millionth of a trillionth of a

Edwin Hubble observing the night sky in 1922, time during which he made his famous discovery about the universe expanding.

LIGHT AND SPEED

Scientists use a figure known as a *light-year* to help them measure the vast distances in our universe. A light-year is the distance light, moving in a vacuum, travels in one year—about 5.9 trillion miles or 186,000 miles per second! Using this figure, we know that light leaving our Sun reaches Earth in 8.3 minutes.

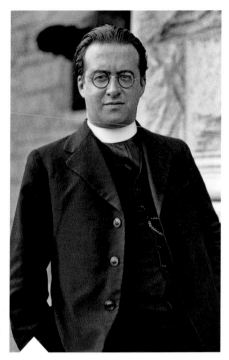

Georges Lemaître in 1933. At the time, he was considered one of the most famous scientists in the world, second only to Albert Einstein.
BETTMANN/CORBIS

GIVING A THEORY A NAME

Sir Fred Hoyle (1915–2001) was a British astronomer who did not believe in Lemaître's hypothesis of the universe erupting from a singularity. In the 1950s Hoyle appeared on a popular British radio show, *The Nature of the Universe*. When he was asked his opinion about the relatively new theory on the origins of the universe, he replied, "Do you mean the big bang?" Hoyle was making fun of the theory, but the name stuck.

trillionth of a second! That unit of measurement is known as Planck time and is represented as 10-43. Named after Max Planck (1858–1947), the German physicist who calculated the measurement, 1 Planck time is the earliest possible instant after the Big Bang that can be determined, and it is when our understanding of the universe begins.

According to the Big Bang theory, the universe quickly expanded from 1 Planck time. And was it hot—ten trillion, trillion times hotter than the core of the Sun! At first the universe was nothing but radiation—energy that is often called the primordial fireball. This fireball was full of the tiniest subatomic particles, called quarks, which in turn formed the earliest atoms. The newborn universe swelled up, and began to cool down. Within three minutes, hydrogen and helium—the most abundant elements in the universe—had formed. During the next million years, gravity pulled the hydrogen and helium into strands called filaments. Around three hundred million years after 1 Planck time, those filaments clumped into clouds of hydrogen and helium and other elements resulting from the Big Bang. Then those clouds came together and formed galaxies, stars, and finally, the planets.

Scientists have been able to explain what happened after the Big Bang, but what happened *before* has remained a nagging question. At this point, most scientists say we simply cannot know. However, remember Mrs. Murry's advice to Meg in *A Wrinkle in Time:* just because something doesn't have an explanation, doesn't mean there isn't one.

For centuries, the age of the universe remained unknown. People could speculate and calculate, but their results were

The Hubble's close-up of some of the oldest galaxies in the universe. They were there long before Earth existed. NASA/ESA/S. Beckwith (STScI) and the HUDF Team

uncertain. The Hubble Space Telescope changed all that. In 1999, Wendy Freedman, an astronomer with the Carnegie Institution for Science, said, "Before Hubble, astronomers could not decide if the universe was ten billion or twenty billion years old." Now that astronomers know the age of the universe, they are able to learn much more about how it began and, perhaps, how it will end. Freedman added, "After all these years, we are finally entering a period of precision cosmology. Now we can more reliably address the broader picture of the universe's origin, evolution, and destiny."

So when did the Big Bang occur? How can science determine the age of the universe? The answers lie in the universe's expansion

THE BIG BOUNCE?

Scientists are always coming up with new hypotheses. In 2007, Martin Bojowald, a physicist working at Pennsylvania State University, proposed an idea explaining what could have happened before the Big Bang. According to Bojowald's hypothesis, our universe may not expand forever. Eventually it could begin contracting, pulling everything in it back into another singularity. That singularity could result in another Big Bang, and a new universe would be born. Furthermore, according to Bojowald, the singularity that became our universe could have been the contraction of a universe that existed before ours. In fact, he suggests the possibility that there could be generations of universes that preceded ours, and generations that will follow, each one bouncing off the singularity that preceded it! Though the theory of the Big Bounce is fascinating, it has not been widely accepted in the scientific community, at least not yet.

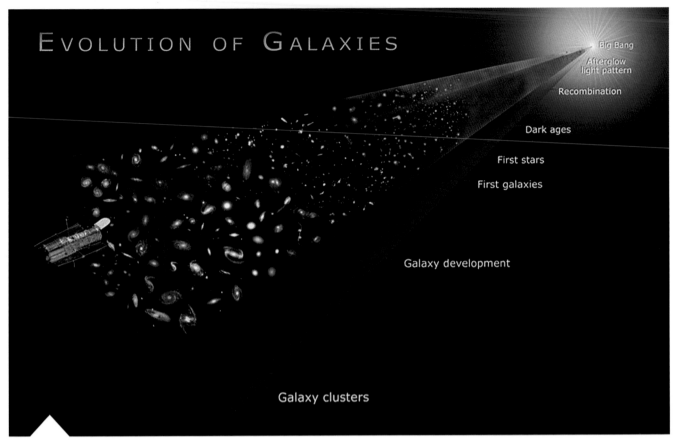

EVOLUTION OF GALAXIES

Big Bang

Afterglow
light pattern

Recombination

Dark ages

First stars

First galaxies

Galaxy development

Galaxy clusters

An illustration showing the cosmic epochs, or ages, of the universe from the Big Bang to the present.
NASA, ESA, AND A. FIELD (STScI)

rate—how fast the galaxies are moving away from one another. We know the faster something goes, the quicker it gets to its destination. Think of a car. If it travels at 60 mph, it will reach its destination faster than if it travels at 30 mph. Speed and time are connected. So if the universe is expanding rapidly, then the galaxies that are farthest away from us would have gotten to where they are quicker than they would have if the universe were expanding slowly. A rapid expansion rate for the universe would indicate that those faraway galaxies are younger than previously thought, because it took them less time to get there.

The Hubble Space Telescope has allowed astronomers to determine that a galaxy appears to gain speed and move away at a rate of 50 miles per second for every 3.2 light-years it is away from Earth. The farther away from Earth it is, the faster it moves—just as Edwin Hubble determined. By using these calculations, and observing the galaxies that are farthest away from us, astronomers now believe our universe is around 13.7 billion years old. If the age of the universe were compared with one 24-hour day, Earth would not have formed until the late afternoon, and humans would have existed for only a few seconds.

EVIDENCE OF THE BIG BANG

Astronomers believe the primordial fireball that immediately followed the Big Bang left a glowing remnant that filled the universe. This telltale glow is called "cosmic microwave background radiation" or CMBR. According to the Big Bang theory, this radiation should be everywhere in the universe. Scientists Arno Penzias and Robert Wilson, working with radio receivers at the Bell Telephone Laboratories in Murray Hill, New Jersey, discovered the existence of cosmic microwave background radiation in 1964. The men heard an annoying hiss in their radios and after ruling out interference from all other sources (and cleaning their antennas from an accumulation of pigeon droppings!) and conducting further studies, they determined that the hiss—which is sometimes called static or noise—was not produced by anything on Earth or even in our solar system. This particular noise was evenly distributed throughout the universe. They had stumbled on the cosmic microwave background radiation that was left over from the Big Bang. In 1978, the men received the Nobel Prize in physics for their discovery.

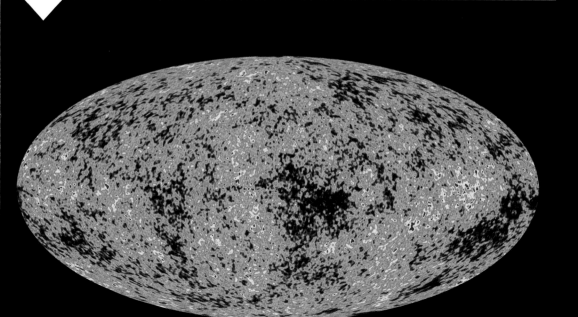

Cosmic microwave background radiation—the oldest light in the universe. This image comes from information collected throughout a period of five years by a space probe called the Wilkinson Microwave Anisotrophy Probe

FOUR

The Dark Forces and Black Holes

There's more to the universe than meets the eye—about 95 percent more, as a matter of fact. Science has revealed that ordinary matter—the stuff of which galaxies, stars, planets, and people are made—accounts for only 5 percent of what exists. The rest neither produces nor reflects light. Essentially, it's invisible. How do scientists know about it, then? Because these mysterious substances, called dark matter and dark energy, have gravity, and gravity always has an effect on the things that surround it, an effect that can be observed.

Stars and galaxies are in constant motion. The stars in individual galaxies orbit around a galaxy's center. Gravity pulls galaxies together into small groups called clusters. The clusters, in turn, orbit around the center of their collection of galaxies. Furthermore, as the universe expands, the swirling clusters of galaxies, like the dots on an inflating balloon, move away from one another as space stretches between them.

The Hubble captures a ghostly ring of dark matter in a cluster of galaxies. This picture, created by Hubble scientists, is a combination of two images. The dark ring is an astronomical map that has been layered on top of the image of the galaxy cluster. The map shows astronomers how the cluster's gravity is distorting the light that is coming to the telescope from more distant galaxies. Discovered in May 2007, this ring is one of the strongest pieces of evidence to date for the existence of the dark matter that scientists believe makes up most of the universe's material.
NASA/ESA, M. J. Jee, and H. Ford (Johns Hopkins University)

29

Fritz Zwicky, working at the California Institute of Technology. He is credited with the discovery of the force that came to be known as dark matter.
AIP EMILIO SERGRE VISUAL ARCHIVES

Dr. Adam Riess, leader of a team of astronomers who discovered dark energy in 1998. W. KIRK, HOMEWOOD PHOTOGRAPHIC SERVICES, JOHNS HOPKINS UNIVERSITY

In the 1930s a Swiss astronomer named Fritz Zwicky (1898–1974) noticed strange behavior in a cluster of galaxies he was studying. Some of the galaxies were whirling around the center of their cluster in an orbit that was so fast, they should have been flung out into the universe, away from their home cluster. Instead, they remained in their group. Something very powerful at the center of the cluster was keeping the racing galaxies in orbit. Zwicky determined that whatever it was had to be massive and have a lot of gravity—more gravity than all the galaxies in the cluster put together. Although he couldn't see it, he knew there was something keeping the galaxies in place, just as one knows the wind—which is not visible—is present when a flag flutters in the breeze. The mysterious substance became known as dark matter.

Astronomers now believe that dark matter surrounds all galaxies and extends out into the universe. Of course, no one knows what dark matter is made of, because no one has ever been able to detect a single particle in it. Still, scientists believe dark matter accounts for about 23 percent of the universe's makeup.

Because of dark matter and its gravitational pull, cosmologists hypothesized that the universe would eventually stop expanding, and might even begin contracting, which could result in something like a Big Crunch—the opposite of the Big Bang—billions of years from now. But they were in for a surprise.

In 1998, Dr. Adam Riess (born 1969), an astrophysicist working at the Space Telescope Science Institute and at Johns Hopkins University, was part of a team that used ground-based telescopes and the Hubble Space Telescope to study the expansion of the universe. "Our aim was to use supernovae—a special kind of exploding star—to measure how fast the universe was expanding in the past and then to compare it with how fast it is expanding now," he said. The team wanted to see if gravity from dark matter was causing the universe to put on the brakes, so to speak, and they wanted to know by how much the expansion was slowing down. They made an unexpected—and astonishing—discovery: The universe is actually speeding up! Dr. Riess said, "If you tossed a ball into the air and it kept right on going up, instead of falling to the ground, you would undoubtedly be very surprised. Well, that's about how surprised we were with this result." The same result was obtained independently by another team of astronomers led by Dr. Saul Perlmutter of the Lawrence Berkeley National Laboratories. Although the pull of dark matter was holding clusters of galaxies together in a group, another invisible force was pushing these cluster groups apart—and pushing them apart fast! This force has been named dark energy, and it remains one of the most studied, yet least understood, forces in the universe.

Research into dark energy and dark matter is just getting under way. The Hubble Space Telescope, along with other observatories, will help scientists look for explanations for these dark mysteries in the universe.

There is another kind of darkness in the universe that has captured imaginations around the world, and become part of our everyday language. When a toy, tool, or other object disappears and cannot be found, often it is said it has fallen into a black hole, meaning it has inexplicably and irretrievably disappeared. Of course, there are no black holes on Earth, and most likely the object in question is findable. But there are black holes in space, and anything that

GRAVITY: HOLDING THINGS TOGETHER

Gravity is the force in the universe that makes all objects pull on, or attract, one another. Objects can be visible matter, such as stars and planets, or they can be invisible, such as dark matter. Scientists now know that visible and invisible matter exert gravity. The more mass, or substance, an object (matter) has, the more gravity it has. On Earth, we know that what goes up, always must come down. Fruit falls from a tree, a baby bird falls from a nest, and a person falls off a bike because Earth is more massive than fruit, a bird, or a person. Earth's gravity pulls everything on Earth toward itself—and gravity is what keeps you from falling off Earth and out into space. Gravity exists throughout the universe.

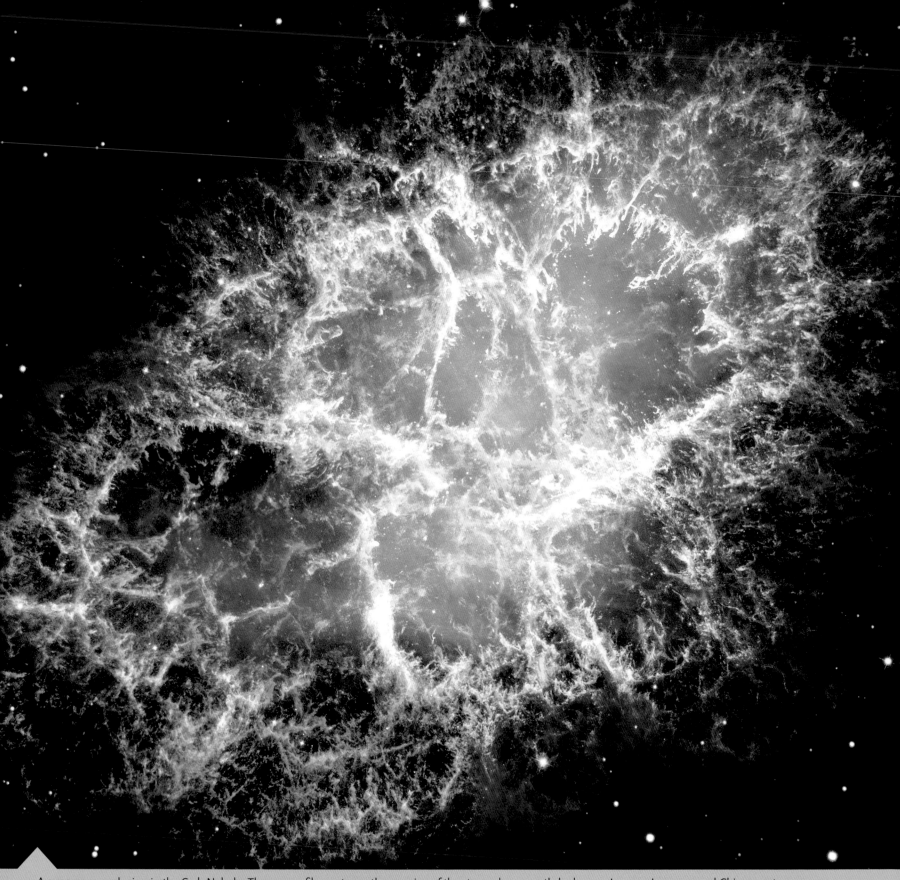

A supernova explosion in the Crab Nebula. The orange filaments are the remains of the star and are mostly hydrogen. In 1054, Japanese and Chinese astronomers recorded this event. The Hubble Space Telescope photographed it in 2005. NASA, ESA, J. HESTER, AND A. LOLL (ARIZONA STATE UNIVERSITY)

disappears into one *is* gone forever. There is no escape from an astronomical black hole, because the pull of its gravity is too strong.

Escaping the force of gravity isn't easy, and the more massive an object is, the harder it is to escape its gravitational pull. For example, during each *Apollo* Moon mission, the rockets carrying the astronauts had to reach 25,000 mph, known as Earth's *escape velocity,* to escape Earth's gravity. When the astronauts left the Moon to return home, their spacecraft had to reach a speed of only 5,300 mph to escape the Moon's gravitational pull. Why? Because the Moon is smaller than Earth and has less mass. Escape velocities are determined by the ratio of an object's mass to its radius—the imaginary line that goes from the center of a sphere to its perimeter. Different objects in the universe have different escape velocities. Nothing in the entire universe is more compact (having a higher ratio of mass to radius) or more compressed than a black hole.

American physicist John Wheeler (1911–2008) gave black holes their name in 1967 in a speech he delivered at the Goddard Institute of Space Studies. It's a clever name, but of course a black hole isn't really a hole. One simplified definition of a black hole is that it's an object whose escape velocity is equal to or exceeds the speed of light. Nothing can go faster than the speed of light; therefore, nothing can escape from a black hole.

One type of black hole forms when the core of a massive star—twenty or more times the size of our Sun—stops fusing light atoms into heavier ones. That fusion process creates nuclear energy, which heats up the gases and makes the star shine. As the dying star, called a supernova, runs out of its nuclear fuel, it explodes in

ORBITS: STAYING CLOSE TO HOME

When the space shuttle *Atlantis* left Earth and carried the astronauts to the Hubble Space Telescope, it was traveling at about 17,500 mph. At that speed, Earth's gravity was still in effect. *Atlantis* did not continue to zoom past the Hubble and out into space. Instead, Earth's gravity pulled the shuttle downward and into a circle that matched the curvature of Earth. After a series of maneuvers, the shuttle moved into the same orbit as the Hubble Space Telescope, and both literally fell into orbit around Earth.

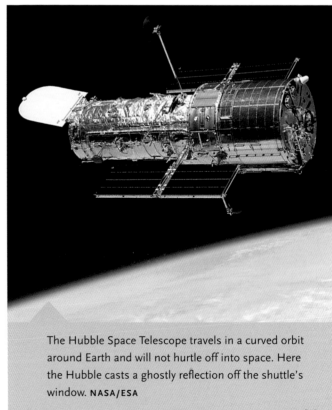

The Hubble Space Telescope travels in a curved orbit around Earth and will not hurtle off into space. Here the Hubble casts a ghostly reflection off the shuttle's window. NASA/ESA

33

John Wheeler in 1973. Note the imaginative drawing of a black hole in the background.
AIP EMILIO SEGRE VISUAL ARCHIVES, WHEELER COLLECTION

a tremendous burst of light and energy, throwing its outer layers into the universe. If less than three times the mass of the star remains in the core after the layers are shed, then the supernova will become a neutron star. Alternatively, if *more* than three times the mass of the star remains after the shedding, the core will keep on collapsing until what is left of the star's mass is packed into one tiny dense point, called, like the cosmic egg that formed the universe, a singularity. Of course, a star's singularity is not the same as the cosmic egg. It contains all the condensed matter from the core of the star, not the entire universe. But the gravity exerted by this super-dense object is strong enough to warp the spacetime that surrounds it.

This warped, bent area around a black hole is called the *event horizon*. Anything that crosses the event horizon—stars, gas, dust,

This artist's image shows a star that has survived the supernova explosion that created a black hole, but its survival will be short-lived. As the star orbits the black hole some of its matter crosses the event horizon and is sucked into it. Right before it disappears, the star's matter emits jets of gas that stream away from the black hole system at 90 percent the speed of light.
ESA/NASA AND FELIX MIRABEL (FRENCH ATOMIC ENERGY COMMISSION AND INSTITUTE FOR ASTRONOMY AND SPACE PHYSICS/CONICET OF ARGENTINA)

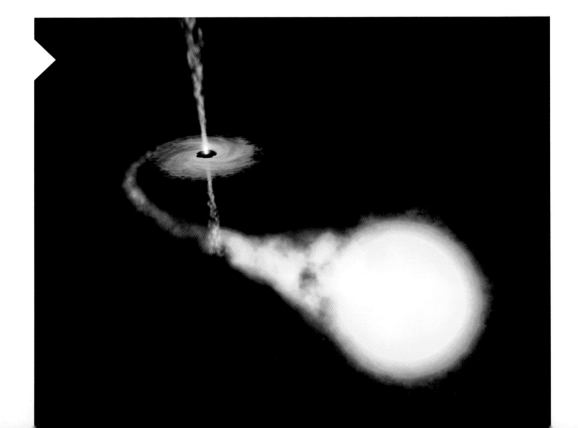

asteroids, and even light—will be drawn into the black hole. In space, anything that comes to the edge of the event horizon will be pulled into the black hole.

Though they weren't called black holes back then, these mysterious areas of space were first noted in the 1790s, when two scientists, John Michell (1724–1793) of England and Pierre-Simon, marquis de Laplace (1749–1827) of France, were studying Newton's laws of motion. Working separately, each man came up with a hypothesis about a possible invisible star in the universe. The hypothesis became a theory, but for centuries no one could find evidence of the existence of these invisible stars, or black holes. The Hubble Space Telescope cannot see black holes, either, but it has photographed the activity that surrounds some of them, evidence that strongly supports their existence.

BENDING SPACETIME

The theory of relativity states, among other things, that spacetime can actually be shaped, or bent, by mass. Picture the surface of a trampoline and think of it as spacetime. If you stand on its surface, your body and its mass will make the trampoline's surface bend inward around your feet. Now imagine someone placing a tennis ball on the edge of the indentation your body has made in the trampoline's surface. That ball will roll inward, toward your feet. It has to happen. But if someone places a tennis ball outside the curve made with your body's mass, the ball will stay put. A black hole's mass works similarly in space, bending it inward to infinity.

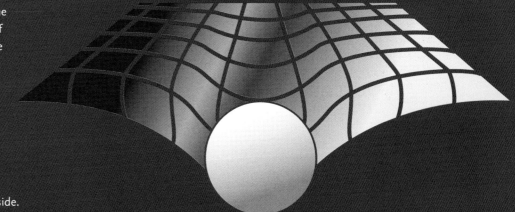

An illustration showing the effect the mass of our Sun has on the surrounding spacetime. Think of spacetime as fabric, capable of being stretched and even torn. Note how the curve of spacetime is steeper near the Sun, and weaker farther away. Note, too, how spacetime is stretched nearer the Sun. All spacetime curves and stretches more when it is close to a mass, and time is slightly different closer to the Sun, though not so much that you would notice it. If the mass is very large, then the dent in spacetime will be very deep. In fact, it can be so deep that the heavy object breaks through spacetime—tears it—and forms a black hole. Nothing escapes from a black hole, and science cannot say what is on the other side.

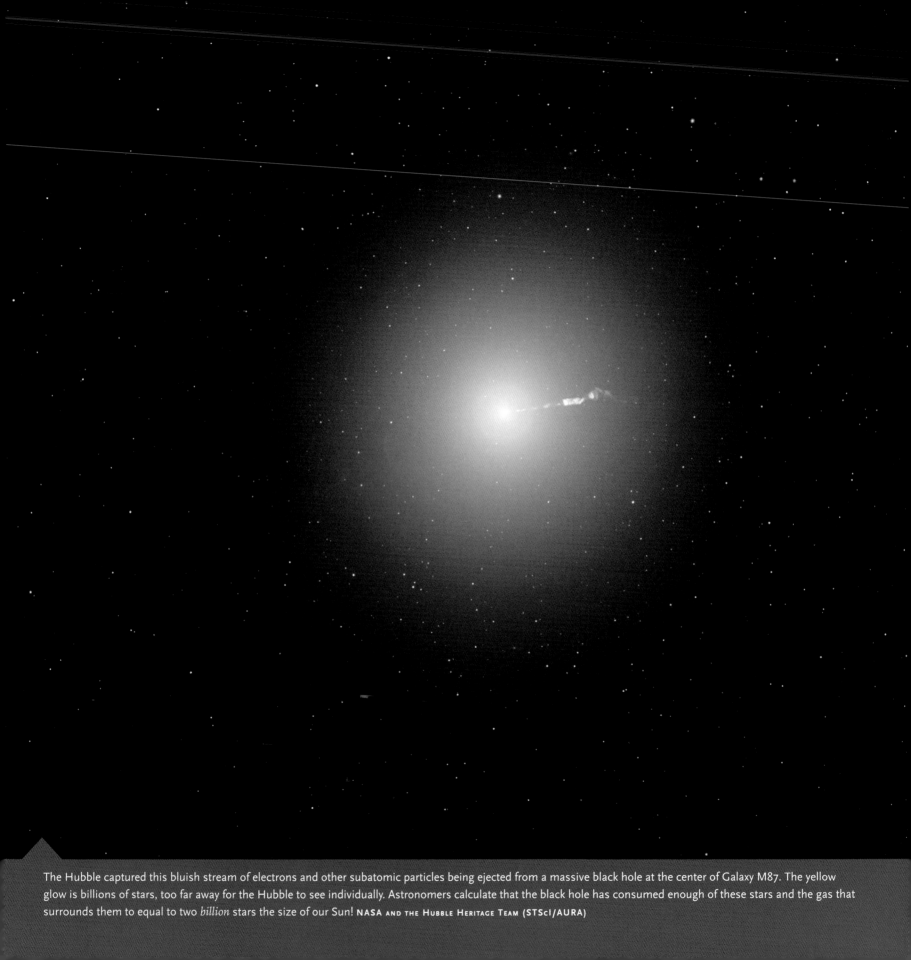

The Hubble captured this bluish stream of electrons and other subatomic particles being ejected from a massive black hole at the center of Galaxy M87. The yellow glow is billions of stars, too far away for the Hubble to see individually. Astronomers calculate that the black hole has consumed enough of these stars and the gas that surrounds them to equal to two *billion* stars the size of our Sun! NASA and the Hubble Heritage Team (STScI/AURA)

An artist's depiction of a star in the process of being destroyed by a black hole. The black hole is pulling on the front of the star more strongly than on the back, stretching the star out and causing its gases to fall into the black hole. M. WEISS, CXC, NASA

One monstrous black hole resides in Messier 87 or M87, an enormous galaxy located fifty million miles away from Earth. Astronomers estimate that it could weigh as much as three *billion* times the mass of our Sun! It was discovered when the Hubble detected a rapid increase in starlight at the center of M87. Astronomers studied the motion of gas at the galaxy's center and concluded that gravity from a massive black hole must be pulling the stars near it inward. As the stars fall into a black hole, they shed their layers of gas, causing brightness. The escaping gas heats up to millions of degrees Fahrenheit and travels at about 99 percent of the speed of light. As it cools, it forms into bubbles approximately 200,000 light-years across, or about twice the diameter of our Milky Way galaxy.

So far, astronomers have detected at least thirteen black holes that are busily gobbling up matter in the Milky Way. However, the closest of these entities is still a whopping 3,000 to 4,000 light-years from Earth. That's far enough away that there's no danger Earth will ever cross any of their event horizons.

FIVE

THE LIFE CYCLE OF A STAR

IF YOU HAVE good eyesight and live in an area where the view of the night sky is not polluted with city lights, you might be able to see, very roughly, about two thousand stars in the sky—though that number may vary. Since Earth is divided into two hemispheres—north and south—your neighbors living in the opposite hemisphere might also be able to see about two thousand stars. So a total of four thousand stars—more or less—are visible from the surface of Earth. However, that is only a tiny percentage of the 100 billion stars in our Milky Way galaxy alone. Multiply that number by at least another 100 billion, and you may come close to the number of stars in the universe. Most of the light in the universe is produced by stars.

Stars have a life cycle—stages of development—just as living things do. Stars are born, they grow to maturity—a period called their *main sequence*—and become old and die. The entire sequence can take millions of years and often much longer.

Thousands of stars are forming within the clouds of rolling gas and dust in this portion of the Orion Nebula. NASA, ESA, AND A. FIELD (STScI)

39

All stars begin their lives in a cloud of space gas—made mostly of hydrogen mixed with grains of space dust—that is called a *nebula*. A nebula is a cloud of gas and dust that glows—usually due to light from nearby stars. Often called "star factories," nebulae are classified according to whether they emit, absorb, or reflect light. Within the nebula, gravity pulls the hydrogen atoms together into a globule of gas that starts to spin. Eventually the spinning creates a central core within the globule of gas, which is heated up by contraction. This heated core is surrounded by a flat, pancake-like disk of leftover dust. When the core's heat reaches about eighteen *million* degrees Fahrenheit, the hydrogen fuses into helium, in a process called nuclear fusion. The star comes to life and begins to glow because of the radiation from the nuclear energy.

It can take anywhere from ten thousand to one million years before nuclear fusion takes place and a star is ready to shine. Once a star reaches this stage, called its main sequence, it continues to convert its supply of hydrogen into helium, depending on its size, for millions—or billions—of years. On Earth, countries have used nuclear fusion to create weapons, but the capacity of explosion of these weapons, tremendous though it may be, is nothing compared with the nuclear fusion inside a star.

When living things die on Earth, they decompose. As they decompose their elements return to the earth, enriching the environment—the soil, the air, the ocean—so new life can begin and established life can continue thriving. So it is with stars. As they die they release material into the cosmos, providing the building blocks for future generations of stars, planets, and perhaps life itself. The atoms that make up our Sun and its solar system, and

The Hubble's instruments captured these stars, packed together in a cluster called NGC 6397. They are located 8,200 light-years away from Earth. The bright blue stars near the center of the cluster are young stars, burning hot and bright. NASA AND THE HUBBLE HERITAGE TEAM (AURA/STScI)

TYPES OF STARS

A star's lifetime is determined by its mass, and a star's mass is determined by the amount of space dust and gas in the nebula in which the star formed. The larger a star is, the shorter its life will be. There are five levels of star formation: very low-mass stars, low-mass stars, intermediate-mass stars, high-mass stars, and very high-mass stars.

▶ **VERY LOW-MASS STARS:** A very low-mass star is called a brown dwarf. Brown dwarfs are stars that fizzled out early in their development. They simply do not have enough mass to fuse hydrogen into helium as a true star does, though they can give off some light and heat. Brown dwarfs are known as substellar objects. In other words, they are not quite stars, but they're close. Brown dwarfs can live for approximately 100 trillion years.

▶ **LOW-MASS STARS:** A low-mass star is a true star, because it produces nuclear fusion. Sometimes called red dwarfs, low-mass stars tend to keep their size all their lives, roughly a trillion years. At the end of its life cycle, it is known as a white dwarf.

▶ **INTERMEDIATE-MASS STARS:** Like all true stars, an intermediate-mass star fuses hydrogen into helium. After it has lived out its mature lifetime, an intermediate-mass star begins to change. As its supply of

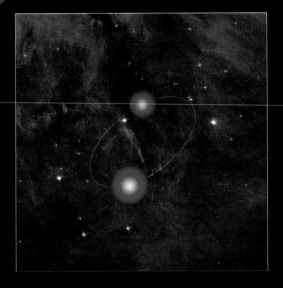

An artist's image of two actual brown dwarfs, mysterious celestial objects that astronomers theorize start out as big as a star, but somehow shrink and cool as they age and end up being closer to the size of a planet. One of these dwarfs is fifty-five times more massive than Jupiter; the other is thirty-five times bigger. In order to burn hydrogen through nuclear fusion and qualify as true stars, the dwarfs would have to be eighty times more massive than Jupiter. An analysis of the light coming from these brown dwarfs showed that the dwarfs had a reddish cast.
NASA/ESA AND A. FELID (STScI)

An artist's concept of red dwarf star CHRX 73 (upper left) and its companion object, CHRX 73 b. Astronomers say the companion object is small enough to be a planet, but also large enough to be a brown dwarf; therefore, they have not decided whether CHRX 73 b is a planet or not. The young star is two million years old and only five hundred light-years away from Earth.
NASA/ESA AND G. BACON (STScI)

The Hubble's cameras took this picture of the remains of a supernova that exploded 160,000 light-years from our own Milky Way galaxy. It is estimated that the star that produced this enormous explosion was fifty times more massive than our Sun. A few million years from now, this gas and dust may be part of the formation of new stars and new planets.
NASA, ESA, HEIC, AND THE **HUBBLE HERITAGE TEAM (STScI/AURA)**

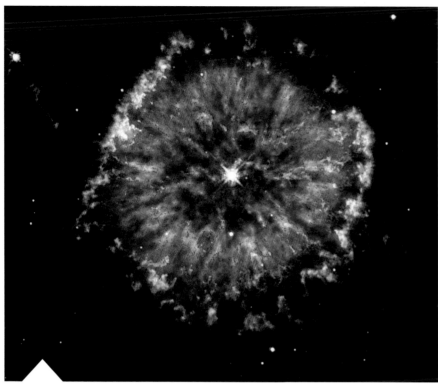

The Hubble took this picture of shells of gas being thrown off by the hot white star at the center of the nebula. Our star, the Sun, is predicted to eject its own planetary nebula around six billion years from now. NASA/THE HUBBLE HERITAGE TEAM (STScI/AURA)

the atoms that make up our own bodies, were once part of a star. In this way, Earth and its people, plants, animals—everything—are literally made of stardust.

Our closest star is the Sun, located 93 million miles away from Earth. Although the Hubble's instruments cannot photograph our own Sun or the planet Mercury (because it is too close to the Sun), they have provided hundreds of amazing images of star birth and death throughout the universe. Two of the new instruments installed on the Hubble during the 2009 mission—the Cosmic Origins Spectrograph and the Wide Field Camera 3—will allow astronomers and other scientists to study the stars with great clarity for years to come.

Continued from page 42.

hydrogen is depleted, it literally runs out of gas. A sudden burst of energy at its core then causes the star to expand and swell, as its outer layers are expelled into the universe as a planetary nebula. The swollen star is now called a red giant. Eventually, the core of a red giant star will contract into a white dwarf. Our Sun is an intermediate-mass star. Astronomers believe the Sun is 4.6 billion years old, and will live for ten billion years, the average life span for this kind of star. Eventually, the Sun will become a red giant.

▶ **VERY HIGH-MASS STARS:** A very high-mass star fuses hydrogen into helium at an extremely fast rate. These huge stars—about a hundred times larger than our Sun—have a relatively short main sequence life of about a million years. As a very high-mass star moves out of its main sequence and the core collapses, the star material that surrounds it is sent flying into space in an explosion called a supernova. A supernova releases more energy in ten seconds than our Sun will produce during its entire ten-billion-year lifetime. The core that remains either becomes a neutron star—the tiniest star of all—or it continues collapsing until it becomes a black hole.

SIX

Recipe for a Planet

Ingredients

You will need:

1 intermediate-mass star

1 nebula containing leftover stardust

millions of pounds gravitational pressure

millions of years' time

Instructions

Using gravitational pressure, whirl nebula containing stardust around the star. Watch until it forms into a flattened, pancake-like disk. Disk will not be uniform or smooth. It will contain large and small clumps of matter. Allow gravity to continue whirling disk around star. Check to see if larger clumps in disk are colliding with smaller clumps. Large clumps should be migrating inward, toward the star, leaving smaller clumps on the

An artist's depiction of the formation of a solar system similar to Earth's. Note the ring of dusty debris— all that remains from the original protoplanetary disk that orbited the star. Closer to the star are orbiting planets.
NASA/JPL-Caltech/T. Pyle/SSC

outer edges. This is normal. Allow process to continue for millions of years. Check disk. Smaller clumps may have disappeared from disk, or become comets, asteroids, and other space debris. Remaining large clumps of matter should now be whirling around central star, each in its own orbit. If so, planets are done.

Yield: Varies, depending on amount of matter in your original nebula. On Earth, the yield is eight planets. Your batch could be larger, or smaller.

Caution: Most planets will be uninhabitable.

Although this recipe is fanciful, it does explain the bare bones of planetary formation. Planets are made from leftovers—the materials remaining after a star has formed. Stars are born in the bits of gas and space dust, or nebulae, that are rotating around them, but not all the material goes into the star's core. After a star begins to shine, the remaining dust, gas, and ice continue swirling around the star and form a flat disk called a *protoplanetary disk*.

Gravity is at work in the protoplanetary disk, just as it is at work in the star. As the disk rotates around the star, gravity causes the particles of dust, ice, and gas to begin sticking together in clumps called *planetesimals*. The bigger the planetesimals get, the more gravity they have. Larger planetesimals attract smaller ones and if they merge, they create objects called *protoplanets*. The protoplanets continue to grow as gravity pulls at their cores, shaping them into spheres, ball-like objects. Sometimes these spheres crash into one another like celestial billiard balls. That kind of action sends smaller objects out of the path of the larger ones and to the outer reaches

The Hubble's cameras took this image of clouds of dust and gas in a small section of the Orion nebula, a region of space that is churning out new stars. The gas is illuminated and heated by ultraviolet light from four hot, massive stars in the nebula. NASA, C. R. O'DELL, AND S. K. WONG (RICE UNIVERSITY)

WHAT IS A PLANET?

The International Astronomical Union is the official body that identifies and names planets. Surprisingly, there had been no official scientific definition for a planet until the IAU decided on one on August 24, 2006. The following definition excludes Pluto from consideration. The IAU defines a planet as a celestial body that

▶ orbits the Sun

▶ is round or almost round

▶ has enough gravity to clear the area around its orbit

of the solar system, where they become dwarf planets, asteroids, and comets. The remaining large spheres become the planets traveling alone in their orbits around their host star.

For centuries, scientists believed our solar system—Earth and its eight planets—to be the only one in the universe. Although astronomers and other scientists had speculated about the existence of other planets, in the 1990s telescopes from the ground and the Hubble Space Telescope aided astronomers in making the first discoveries of other planets orbiting other stars outside our solar system. Those planets are called *exoplanets*.

Even before the Hubble was launched, in the 1980s, some astronomers hypothesized that a star in the southern constellation of Pices Australis, or the Southern Fish, might have a planet or two in its orbit. The star's name was Fomalhaut, which means "whale's mouth" in Arabic, and it is the brightest star in its constellation. In 2004, an instrument onboard the Hubble called the Advanced Camera for Surveys (ACS) detected an enormous protoplanetary

In 2006, the Hubble Space Telescope's instruments detected the presence of this Jupiter-sized planet orbiting a young (eight hundred million years!) star in our galaxy. At 10.5 light-years away, it is the closest planet outside those of our solar system. This is an artist's concept of what the planet looks like, since its star is still surrounded by a disk of dust that extends into space twenty billion miles. Hubble could only detect the planet's presence by measuring the gravitational pull, or tug, it had on its star.
NASA/ESA AND G. BACON (STScI)

disk, 21.5 *billion* miles across, in orbit around Fomalhaut. In 2005, the Hubble's cameras were able to capture an actual image of the protoplanetary disk.

Paul Kalas, an astronomer working at the University of California, Berkeley, along with a team of other astronomers, suggested that gravity—and therefore a mass—was tugging on the disk. Scientists wondered whether the gravity of a planet was pulling on it. Finally, in November 2008, they discovered that there was a planet orbiting Fomalhaut. The Hubble's cameras photographed it. The planet, which is three times the size of Jupiter, was named Fomalhaut b.

It takes time and patience to be a scientific planet hunter. Paul Kalas said, "Our Hubble observations were incredibly demanding. Fomalhaut b is one billion times fainter than the star. We began this program in 2001 and our persistence has finally paid off." His team member Mark Clampin of NASA's Goddard Space Flight Center added, "The lesson for exoplanet hunters is 'follow the dust.'"

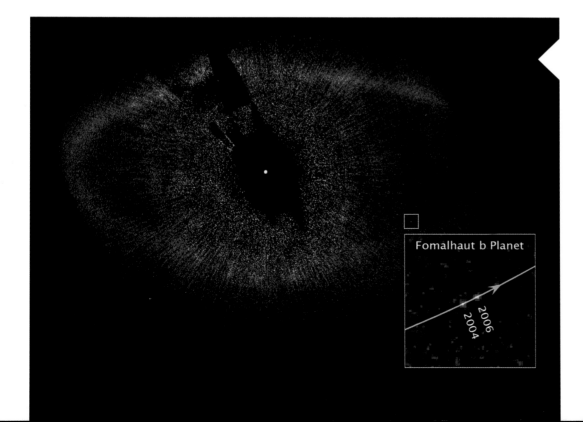

Fomalhaut b Planet

2006
2004

The Hubble captured the star Fomalhaut surrounded by its protoplanetary disk. Inside the disk to the right, the planet Fomalhaut b has formed and is in orbit. Astronomers use movement to detect the presence of exoplanets. Note the movement of Fomalhaut b from 2004 to 2006. **NASA, ESA, AND P. KALAS (UNIVERSITY OF CALIFORNIA, BERKELEY)**

Although Fomalhaut is an intermediate-mass star, it is much larger than our Sun—and much brighter, too. In fact, Fomalhaut, which is located in the southern hemisphere, is the seventeenth brightest star in the night sky. Fomalhaut is a very young star—about one hundred to three hundred million years old. It is burning its hydrogen so fast that astronomers think it will burn out in about one billion years. That's a short life span for a star, mostly likely not enough time to give life any chance to develop on Fomalhaut b.

That does not mean some form of life could not exist on one of the many hundred other exoplanets that have been discovered with the help of the Hubble since 1995. Like Fomalhaut b, most have been large Jupiter-like gas giants, not rocky terrestrial planets like Earth. To support life, a planet would have to have the right conditions to store carbon, oxygen, hydrogen, and nitrogen, the chemical building blocks necessary for life, as we know it, to exist. The planet would also have to have a source of liquid water, and be the right distance from its star so it would be neither too hot nor too cold. It would need the right atmosphere of gases to support life, too. In other words, it would have to be pretty similar to Earth.

So far, out of the hundreds of billions of stars in the universe, no one has found another Earth. But that doesn't mean one doesn't exist, or that, aided by the Hubble, scientists won't be able to find it.

As the characters in *A Wrinkle in Time* discovered, our universe is a wondrous place. And while it is mysterious to be sure, solving its mysteries is now within the realm of possibility.

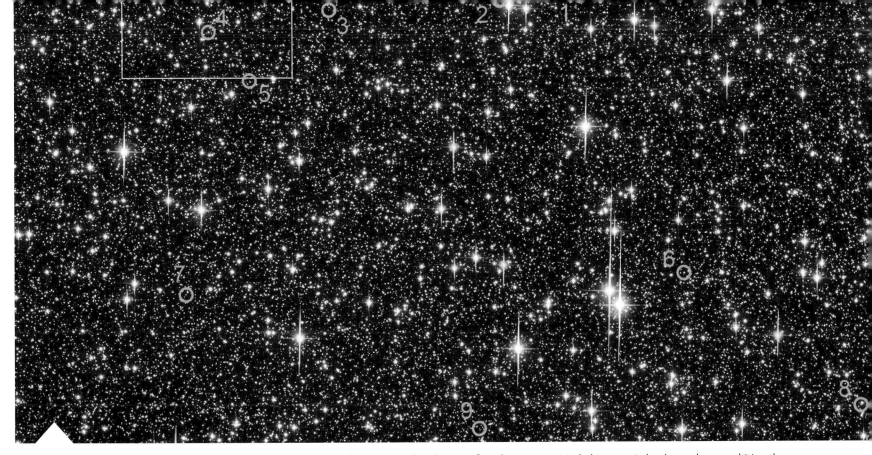

The Hubble's instruments searched this field of stars, looking for planets. The telescope found nine stars (circled in green) that have planets orbiting them. Astronomers can detect the presence of a planet by observing the gravity it exerts on its star as it orbits. Gravity tugs on the star, causing it to wobble. Astronomers can also detect a planet in orbit when it eclipses, or passes in front of, its star, partially blocking out its light. Astronomical instruments can measure the frequency of the eclipses, and determine if an object like a planet is in orbit around the star. Only time will tell if another Earth-like planet is out there somewhere. THE HUBBLE HERITAGE TEAM (AURA/STScI/NASA)

As humans, we will continue to study the cosmos and wonder: Where did we come from? What is our fate? Are there others out there, asking the same questions we ask? As science moves forward, each generation will ask more questions and make more discoveries than the generation preceding it. The body of knowledge will grow as we seek scientific answers to the question of *how* the universe came to be the way it is.

Why the universe exists is an entirely different question—one that science cannot answer. We each must answer that question for ourselves.

AFTERWORD

AFTER 12 days, 21 hours, and 37 minutes in space, the crew of STS-125 finally returned to Earth, their mission complete. At a welcome home ceremony at the Johnson Space Center, "Hubble Hugger" John Grunsfeld said, "Hubble is an evolving story . . . that story isn't at the end with the termination of our mission. It's really the beginning of a brand new Hubble story. We're looking forward to the great science that will come out of Hubble."

In the afterglow of the successfully completed mission, however, there was a three-month wait before anyone could begin to use the telescope once again. The new instruments onboard the Hubble had to go through a process called outgassing. Despite every effort to keep the Hubble instruments sterile while they were on Earth, there was some contamination—molecules of earthly gas attached themselves to the instruments and traveled into space with them. Because even one molecule of unwanted gas could interfere with the instruments' ability to function, everyone had to

One of the Hubble's first images after the servicing mission shows a gas jet in the Carina Nebula.
NASA, ESA, AND THE HUBBLE SM4 ERO TEAM

wait for several weeks while outgassing—allowing the unwanted molecules to simply float away into space—took place.

Additionally, small parts within the instruments were out of alignment. When instruments went from having weight on Earth to being weightless in space, small mirrors inside them moved slightly. Engineers on Earth were able to gently shift the mirrors back into their proper positions via computers connected to the Hubble. This process also took a few weeks.

Finally, the instruments had to be calibrated. When an instrument is calibrated, it is adjusted to match a given norm. For example, if you wanted to make sure a bathroom scale was accurate, you could put a ten-pound weight on it, and check to see if the scale registered exactly ten pounds. If the scale read 10.2 pounds, you would know it needed to be adjusted, or calibrated, to read the correct weight.

Astronomers calibrated the Hubble's instruments by measuring their data, or information, against a known astronomical value. Instead of the ten-pound weight used to calibrate the bathroom scale, the astronomers compared the instruments' readings with past observations they knew were accurate. They carefully adjusted the Hubble's instruments to ensure that any new observations would be absolutely precise and the images completely clear.

At last, in September 2009, the Hubble was ready to show off its new capabilities. The pressroom at NASA headquarters was crowded with reporters eager to see what the Hubble saw. Others all over the world tuned in as well. Ten million hits came into the

These are the first images that were released after the Hubble was repaired. They include a butterfly-shaped nebula (opposite) and a densely packed cluster of stars (p. 56). **NASA/ESA AND THE HUBBLE SM4 ERO TEAM**

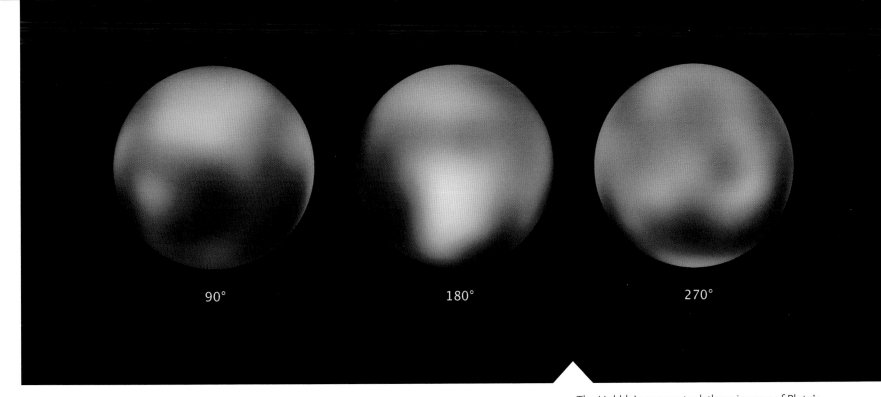

90°   180°   270°

The Hubble's camera took these images of Pluto's surface—the most detailed that have ever been seen of the dwarf planet. The photographs show seasonal changes, as Pluto goes through its 248-year-long orbit of the Sun. **NASA**

computer server at Space Telescope Science Institute, slowing it down for two days. "Not that we minded," said Rachel Osten, an astronomer at the institute. "We all knew the reason why!"

In Washington, D.C., Edward Weiler, associate administrator for NASA's Science Mission Directorate, said, "This marks a new beginning for Hubble. The telescope was given an extreme make-over and now is significantly more powerful than ever, well equipped to last into the next decade." Maryland senator Barbara Mikulski, who had worked to make the Hubble mission happen, said, "I fought for the Hubble repair mission because Hubble is the people's telescope. I also fought for Hubble because it constantly rewrites the science textbooks. It has more discoveries than any other science mission. Hubble is our greatest example of our astronauts working together with scientists to show American leadership and ingenuity."

The upgraded Hubble Space Telescope released this image of hundreds of brilliant blue stars. Several of these stars are one hundred times more massive than our Sun.

NASA/ESA, F. Paresce (NAF-IASF, Bologna, Italy), R. O'Connell (University of Virginia, Charlottesville), and the Wide Field Camera 3 Science Oversight Committee

Astronomers, astronauts, and everyone else who is curious about the universe will continue to follow the Hubble's discoveries until the great observatory comes to the end of its useful life, probably around or just before 2020. No further repair missions are scheduled for it.

Fortunately, another great observatory, the James Webb Space Telescope, is waiting to be launched in 2014. Named after a former administrator of NASA, the James Webb is being constructed to see in the infrared wavelengths in an area of space much farther from Earth than the Hubble can, where there is a constant magnetic field. The James Webb will be used to study four scientific themes: the end of the Dark Ages and First Light in the universe, the assembly of galaxies, the birth of stars and protoplanetary systems, and planetary systems and the origins of life. It will continue the work the Hubble began, casting a probing eye upon the universe, so we can continue to appreciate its beauty and uncover more of its deepest mysteries.

USING THE HUBBLE

Astronomers and others working at the Space Telescope Science Institute (STScI) in Baltimore, Maryland, do a lot of observing with the Hubble, but they also make it available to other astronomers around the world. Each year, the institute receives around one thousand requests, asking permission to use the Hubble. These requests are made in the form of proposals, which say—among other things—what area of the sky astronomers want to observe and the purpose of their observations—what it is they are hoping to discover. The proposals are submitted to STScI and evaluated by an international panel of scientists. There are usually six requests for every proposal granted, so getting an opportunity to use the Hubble is a competitive endeavor! The Hubble works twenty-four hours a day, seven days a week. Because of its heavy workload, on average, more than eight scientific papers per week are published based on its observations. In addition, astronomers and others present their findings at scientific conferences around the world, so everyone benefits from this remarkable scientific instrument. Because of the success of STS-125, astronomers can make their observations with the upgraded Hubble in a fraction of the time that was needed before. Therefore, more observations will be possible well into the future.

GLOSSARY

ASTRONAUT: A person trained to take part in a space flight.

ASTRONOMY: The study of stars, planets, and other celestial bodies outside Earth's atmosphere.

ASTROPHYSICIST: An astronomer who studies the behavior and physical properties of celestial bodies and phenomena.

ATMOSPHERE: The gases surrounding the surface of a planet, moon, or star.

ATOM: The smallest unit, or part, of any chemical element.

BIG BANG THEORY: A theory that states the universe erupted from a singularity, or cosmic egg.

BLACK HOLE: A celestial object that has a gravitational field so strong, nothing, not even light, can escape.

CAPE CANAVERAL: Launch site in eastern Florida of the United States' space flights.

COSMIC BACKGROUND RADIATION: Radiation that filled the universe after the Big Bang and is still detectable.

COSMIC EGG: The singularity that contained all the matter of the universe before the Big Bang.

DARK ENERGY: A mysterious force that is pushing galaxies apart and thought to be the cause of the accelerating expansion of the universe.

DARK MATTER: A mysterious substance that accounts for 23 percent of the universe. It is not visible or directly detectable but has gravitational pull.

ESCAPE VELOCITY: The speed required to exit the gravitational pull of a planet or moon.

EVENT HORIZON: The area that borders a black hole. Once an object crosses the event horizon, it will be sucked into the black hole.

EXOPLANETS: Planets orbiting other stars outside our solar system.

GALAXY: A massive cluster of stars, planets, and other matter held together by gravity.

GRAVITY: The force of attraction all bodies of mass in the universe possess. The larger the body, the more gravity it has.

HELIUM: A colorless, odorless gas that is the second lightest and the second most abundant element in the universe.

HUBBLE CONSTANT: An equation that uses the speed of light to calculate the expansion rate of the universe.

HUBBLE SPACE TELESCOPE: NASA's first orbiting observatory, placed in orbit above Earth's atmosphere in April 1990. It has been called the greatest scientific instrument of all time.

HUBBLE'S LAW: The statement that the distance between galaxies and clusters of galaxies is continuously increasing and therefore the universe is expanding.

HYDROGEN: A colorless, odorless gas that is the lightest and most abundant element in the universe.

HYPOTHESIS: A proposed scientific explanation based on observation.

INTERNATIONAL SPACE STATION: Orbiting scientific laboratory launched in 1998 and constructed and managed by the United States, Canada, Japan, Russia, the eleven nations of the European Space Agency, and Brazil. At any given time, two to three astronauts live on the space station for up to six months, doing research and conducting experiments.

JAMES WEBB SPACE TELESCOPE: A space telescope that will be launched in 2014.

LAW: In science, a general statement that describes regularly repeating facts or events.

LIGHT-YEAR: The distance light travels in a year, about 6 trillion miles.

MATTER: Any substance in the universe that takes up space and has mass; matter can be liquid, solid, or gas.

MILKY WAY: The galaxy that is home to Earth's solar system.

NEBULA: An interstellar cloud of gas and dust.

OBSERVATION: In science, the act of watching and studying the behavior of an object or phenomenon over a period of time.

OBSERVATORY: A building or structure that houses equipment to study the stars, planets, and other celestial objects. Space telescopes such as the Hubble Space Telescope and the James Webb Space Telescope are frequently referred to as observatories.

ORBIT: The curved path one object takes as it revolves around another.

PLANCK TIME: The first measurable moment of the universe. Written as 10-43.

PLANET: A large, round celestial body that occupies its own orbit around a star and has cleared the neighborhood around its orbit of other bodies.

PROTOPLANETARY DISK: The leftover material from a star's formation that forms into a disk orbiting its star. Planets can be formed from these materials.

PROTOPLANETS: A small celestial object roughly the size of a moon, formed from dust and other particles that have collided and stuck together. Some protoplanets continue to gain mass until they form planets.

ROBOTIC ARM: A boom attached to the space shuttle.

SHUTTLE: A reusable space plane used for carrying astronauts and cargo between Earth and space.

SINGULARITY: An incredibly hot, dense point of matter, to which the laws of physics no longer apply.

SOLAR SYSTEM: A star and the collection of planets and other bodies that orbit it.

SPACE: The part of the universe beyond Earth's atmosphere.

SPACE TELESCOPE SCIENCE INSTITUTE: The Space Telescope Science Institute, or STScI, is responsible for administering the scientific work done with the Hubble Space Telescope and with the new James Webb Space Telescope.

SPACEWALK: Activity astronauts conduct in space while outside a space shuttle or the International Space Station.

SPECTRUM: A continuum of color formed when white light is broken into its component colors, or wavelengths.

SPEED OF LIGHT: Approximately 186,000 miles per second.

STAR: A celestial body that shines through the release of energy caused by nuclear reaction.

SUPERNOVA: A stellar explosion that occurs at the end of some stars' life cycles and is extremely bright.

TELESCOPE: An instrument that uses lenses, mirrors, or a combination of lenses and mirrors to make distant objects appear larger and closer.

THEORY: A statement based on a hypothesis that has not been disproved after testing and is generally agreed to be true.

UNIVERSE: All existing things, including all matter and all energy, on Earth and in space.

FOR FURTHER READING

BOOKS

Fleisher, Paul. *The Big Bang*. Minneapolis: Twenty-First Century Books, 2005.

Jackson, Ellen. *The Mysterious Universe*. Boston: Houghton Mifflin Company, 2008.

L'Engle, Madeleine. *A Wrinkle in Time*. New York: Fararr, Straus and Giroux, 1962.

Miller, Ron. *Satellites*. Minneapolis: Twenty-First Century Books, 2007.

Rhatigan, Joe, Rain Newcomb, and Greg Doppmann. *Out-of-This-World Astronomy*. New York: Sterling Publishing, 2005.

Thomson, Sarah L. *Extreme Stars! Q & A*. New York: HarperCollins, 2006.

Wright, Kenneth. *Scholastic Atlas of Space*. New York: Scholastic, 2005.

WEBSITES OF INTEREST

Amazing Space *amazing-space-stsci.edu*

Astronomy Picture of the Day *antwrp.gsfc.nasa.gov*

Hubble Space Telescope *hubblesite.org*

James Webb Space Telescope *jwst.nasa.gov*

National Aeronautics and Space Administration *www.nasa.gov*

Star Child: A Learning Center for Young Astronomers *starchild.gsfc.nasa.gov*

Far flung galaxies, captured by the newly repaired Hubble. NASA/ESA, AND THE HUBBLE SM4 ERO TEAM

INDEX

NOTE: Page numbers in **bold type** refer to illustrations.